HOW TO CHANGE YOUR UNIVERSE

A practical guide to living the greatest life possible – in the greatest
world possible

JON GABRIEL

Published by:

The Gabriel Method Pty Ltd.

P.O. Box 5422, Albany, WA 6332, Australia

Website: thegabrielmethod.com

For a free powerful visualization, visit thegabrielmethod.com/bestworld

Edited by Xavier Waterkeyn

Addendum – *You Will Live Forever* by Inge Tatiana

Content from Chapters 9, 10 and 12 reprinted with permission from *Visualization For Weight Loss* by Jon Gabriel © 2015 Hay House, Carlsbad, CA.

A catalogue record for this work is available from the National Library of Australia

ISBN 9780646833941 (paperback)

ISBN 9780646834726 (EPUB)

For a free powerful visualization, visit
thegabrielmethod.com/bestworld

To Inge and Leo

I wrote this book for you, to give you the most essential tools to let you thrive and prosper in this world and any other.

CONTENTS

VIRTUAL REALITY

1

UNIVERSE HOPPING

ON JANUARY 10, 2006, an hour before midnight, I died.

At least I think I did. I'm not sure.

I had been writing since 4:00 in the morning nonstop. It was a cathartic experience, where I felt like I was cleansing all of the emotional pain and trauma I'd endured over the last 15 years.

Five days earlier I had just finished a massive physical cleanse, where I had taken nothing but water for 21 days. Now, even after the cleanse, I'd had no appetite whatsoever. There was a box of persimmons on the table and I occasionally ate one as I was passing by, but food had completely left my thoughts.

I had totally purified my body on a physical level, and now I was experiencing a kind of emotional purification.

But at 11:00 pm, I leaned back on my chair and I left my body. I was floating behind my body and looking at it. It appeared to me that I had stopped breathing.

I woke up the next morning in the same position, and yet I was a completely different person. I was in a superconscious state. It's almost impossible for me to describe what I experienced that day, but I'll try.

I felt like my awareness had expanded, not only to every corner of the earth, but to every corner of the universe. I felt that I had complete knowledge and awareness of everything that was going on in the universe at once and not only *this* universe. I felt that *this* universe was nothing more than a tiny cell in my body and that there were as many universes as there are cells in my body. There were trillions and trillions of universes and, in an unexplainable way, I had an awareness of every single one of them.

It was almost like I was a being who was made up of an infinite number of universes. And, somehow, I had awareness of everything that was happening in *all* of them.

And the joy and the beauty and the ecstasy that I felt running through my body is simply indescribable. I was in a state of constant joy. It was impossible for me to feel stress or pain or worry about any of life's dramas. I felt that life would never trouble me again.

I had become, in some way, enlightened and I thought it would be like this forever.

And every encounter I had was transformative for the person I was speaking with.

I remember speaking to a lady at the store, a friend of mine that I bumped into. She was worried about something.

As I was talking with her, I could see her energy flowing through her body. It appeared as a white light moving through her body. In some places it was yellow.

I could also see her entire future, like a timeline. Everything that she would ever do and everything that would even happen to her was all laid out in front of me. I could see her entire past too.

From my perspective, her past was on the left side of her and her future was on the right.

She was upset about certain things in her life and wanted to be in a different situation. I then saw the version of her that could accomplish the things she wanted to do and be the person she wanted to be. That timeline, her *ideal scenario*, her *ideal life*, existed in a higher energy state, parallel to her current timeline. I could see it 'on top of' or 'overlaid' on her current past-present-future, existing simultaneously as an *alternate* past-present-future.

In order to achieve this version of herself, I could see she would have to *be* in a higher vibrational state. She would have to *become* a higher energy version of herself.

As I was looking at the energy flowing through her body, I could see she had a block in her energy channels on the left side of her abdomen. I could see that this block was caused by some sort of emotional trauma. This block was weighing her down, 'anchoring' her to her current less-than-ideal life and stopping her from being in that higher energy state. Because her energy couldn't flow properly, her energy was restricted, causing her to be in a lower vibrational state.

As I was talking with her, part of my mind was focused on trying to unblock her energy channels.

The blockage opened up and her energy started flowing freely and she started crying profusely. Ostensibly, she was crying because of something that had happened in the conversation. But I knew that she was crying because she had had an emotionally cathartic experience, that she had worked through a trauma that had manifested as a block. Once the block was gone and her energy could flow more freely, her energy started vibrating at a higher frequency.

As we were there talking together, I saw her transition into that higher energy timeline. She now had a completely different future than the one that I had just seen.

Just as amazing is that she now had a different past too!

Both her *past* and *future* had changed.

She was now in a different timeline, a slightly different universe, but with very different outcomes and experiences waiting for her, and I knew she'd never be the same again. She was crying profusely, and she was hugging me.

Each of my encounters had this sort of transformative effect, and people I knew were hugging me and crying wherever I went.

This experience of superconsciousness lasted for five days. And after five days, this state of superconsciousness was gone and I was plunged from the highest states of heaven to the lowest states of hell, literally overnight.

I was devastated. Not only was I devastated emotionally, I was devastated physically. My body simply could not handle the intensity of the energy that was coursing through it.

Since then, I've spent these subsequent years purifying my body through fasting and clean eating, healing emotional traumas and doing meditation, visualization and other practices to open my energy channels as much as possible, so that I can manifest more and more of this divine energy – an energy that had once *fully* expressed itself through me, albeit for a very short time.

And, over time, I've come to feel more and more of that energy able to express itself through my body. Every time that I'm able to open up my energy channels more, it allows more of this energy to enter my body and express itself through me. And every time that more of this energy can express itself through me, my life changes in positive ways and so does the rest of the world too.

Whenever I have problems in my life, I always focus my awareness inside to solve the problem. I focus on my energy channels, my state of vibration, on healing past traumas and correcting dysfunctional beliefs – all the things that I've come to learn will get to the *root* of the 'problem', not just the external appearance of 'the problem', or the way that 'the problem' shows up.

Because I've also come to learn that the problem is ALWAYS me and my ability to channel energy into the world. If I'm blocked *energetically*, it will show up as a blockage in my life – a problem in my health, relationships, business or sometimes even a problem in the so-called 'exterior world' – the world at large. When I unblock and can channel more energy, *my vibration rises*, and the problem goes away.

While most memories fade over time, the experience of becoming a superbeing for five days seems to get more and more vivid and I'm able to assimilate more and more of what I learned from that experience, so many years ago.

What I learned and what I continue to realize is that there are an infinite number of universes and we're moving through these universes all the time, depending on our energy and our vibration and other factors that we'll talk about in this book.

Over the last few years, I have been studying quantum physics and I was excited to see that modern-day physics has, to some extent, caught up with this idea of multiple universes and our relationship to them. The idea that we live in a 'multiverse' or 'omniverse' with an infinite number of 'parallel' universes is no longer just a theory.

Quantum Immortality

Hugh Everett was the first person to propose the 'many worlds' theory in physics. This is the idea that there are an infinite number of worlds existing simultaneously. He was also a believer in something called 'quantum immortality' which states that consciousness is independent of what we think of as 'physical reality' and it's not tied to the 'particles' that make up our bodies. Everett believed, as I do, that our consciousness not only *can* move from one world or timeline to another, but actually *does* move from one timeline to another, from one universe to another, *all the time*, without us even knowing, almost like changing the channels on the TV.

He proposed the 'many worlds' theory back in the 1950s. He was a graduate student at the time and never actually became a physicist because his ideas were so radical that he was laughed at and ridiculed by his peers. Fast forward 70 years later and his name and theories are now being talked about as much as any great physicist in history. So it goes ...

Today scientists argue about the exact number of universes that exist. Are there infinite universes, or just a very large number of them? Some have estimated that at the 'moment of creation', there were ten to the five hundredth other universes created. That's one with 500 zeros after it. That's trillions and trillions of times more universes than there are atoms in the 'single observable universe' that we can detect all around us. The difference between one universe and another might be as little as the position of a solitary grain of sand on a beach. Many of these universes are so similar that you wouldn't even be able to know that you moved from one to the other, except for very subtle differences in the way you might remember the past.

A lot of people talk about the law of attraction: how when you visualize what you want and you use affirmations and visualizations, you're actually *creating* or *attracting* to you the thing that you want.

Well, in my experience, that's not exactly what's going on.

What's really going on is that there are infinite versions of you, experiencing an infinite number of different scenarios. There's a version of you that has the exact career you want, the abundance and prosperity you would love to have and the right relationships. There's a version of you where you're living in a world with no war, no pollution, clean energy, no crime and food for everyone.

There's a version of you – in fact, an infinite number of versions of you – where you're 'having it all'.

When you successfully use the so-called 'laws of attraction' to achieve something, you haven't 'created' that thing or 'attracted' it to you. It already existed as a 'state' in a pre-existing universe and what happened is that YOU simply transitioned to that 'new' universe, where that state of affairs is happening.

Jack Canfield, author of *Chicken Soup for The Soul*, who was one of the people in the movie *The Secret*, talked about how he visualized selling one hundred thousand copies of his book in one year, and how that happened. I would argue that he didn't actually 'manifest' that experience. There was just a huge number of universes in which a version of him sold one hundred thousand copies of his book in one year and he left the 'Jack Canfield, nice guy who wrote a book' universe that he was in and transitioned to one of the many 'Jack Canfield, best-selling author' universes.

What my 'dying and being reborn' experience showed me is that we – all of us – are constant universe travelers. We move without even being aware of it. We're traveling from one universe to another all the time. We're constantly transitioning, and for the most part, we're transitioning unconsciously.

But I say, "Let's travel consciously!"

Let's become *conscious* explorers of the omniverse as we transition from one universe to another. Let's *consciously* find our way to the greatest universes that are possible for us, where we can have the most amazing lives that are possible, in the most perfect of possible worlds.

Right now, this may sound incredibly ridiculous and inconceivable to you. But consider this: Google and the Department of Defense are spending hundreds of millions of dollars to create quantum computers – computers that take advantage of parallel universes!

The richest, most powerful organizations in the world are using parallel universes to help them solve problems. In October 2019, Google's quantum computer solved a problem in three and a half minutes that would have taken the best standard computers ten thousand years to solve. This computer did it in *less than four minutes!*

You might think that the idea that we are traveling through universes without knowing it is totally crazy and unfathomable and ridiculous. You might think, "This is stupid! I know what I know. I know what's real!"

But I'm inviting you to entertain the idea that there is an underlying reality that's deeper than the one you think you live in. I'm inviting you to take a deep dive into what's really going on out there in a 'real' world that is more real than the world you think you know – the 'reality' that our senses and our minds are telling us exist. I'm inviting you to see that an omniverse of infinite or virtually infinite universes is not only possible, but true.

It's not only possible, it's incredibly likely that you and I are universe travelers. We are adventurers transitioning from universe to universe. It's happening all the time based on our energy and our vibration, our frequency, our expectations, our programming and lots of other things.

It's happening without us realizing it. But we *can* become conscious of the process and move purposefully! We can consciously change our intentions, our vibrations, our programing, our expectations, and we can consciously transition into the best universe possible for us.

I realize this is a HUGE paradigm shift, but there's something very empowering about this paradigm. Think of all the problems in the world and how small and powerless we sometimes feel to solve them. What if all the solutions to all of your problems and all of the world's problems ALREADY EXISTS? What if the answers exist in another universe, just waiting for us?

We don't need anything from anyone to 'solve' these problems. We don't need to *solve* anything. It's just up to us to *access* a new reality. We just have to understand how to *consciously* transition into the highest worlds possible. The only control we need is the conscious control to navigate our way to those worlds – and it's all within our own control!

We have all the power in the world to 'change' our world, not by manipulating our world or 'attracting' something to our world, but because we can *exchange* one universe for another. We can go to the universe where the change has already occurred. We can go to the universe where things are working out better – where things have *always* been working out better, where we are finding solutions, where we have *already* found solutions, solutions for clean energy, pollution, toxins, peace, world hunger and countless other problems.

All the problems you want to solve in your life and in the world you can solve by going to the world where the solutions already exist. That means that all the power to change the world and to change your life is inside of you! No one can give it to you, and no one can take it away – and that's an incredibly powerful notion.

Maybe you won't be able to solve all your problems and the world's problems instantly, because your ability to move from one universe to another might be limited by certain factors, such as limiting beliefs, emotional blockages and how much energy your body can channel at any given time. Getting to a point where you can work through the limitations, and where you can freely channel energy and experience higher vibrations, is a *process*.

But what I'd like to introduce you to is an understanding that:

1. The world you think is real is nothing of the sort.
2. The world you think you know is one of a virtually infinite number of worlds.
3. That you've spent your life moving through these worlds, blindly and reactively.
4. That you can move through these worlds with purpose and intent.
5. You can move through these worlds consciously and with greater and greater freedom once you understand some core principles – laws of universal transitioning, if you like.

In this book I hope to give you an understanding of these principles and what you need to do to raise your energy and your vibration to continually rise higher and higher and get closer and closer to reaching the most perfect desired outcomes for yourself, your loved ones and the world.

The steps are simple, powerful and effective and become more powerful and more effective over time, with practice.

And so I would invite you to come with me, take this adventure and be travelers with me, conscious travelers, consciously moving from universe to universe and consciously improving ourselves and our world and our experiences through taking the steps and actions that we'll talk about in this book.

2

SEEING IS BELIEVING – BUT IT DEFINITELY SHOULDN'T BE!

IN ORDER TO understand how it's possible that we can be moving from universe to universe without knowing it, let's start by looking at what it is we actually think we know.

We might think we're real, solid beings, living in a real solid world – a solidity that we can count on because we feel that solidity with everything that we touch. A world that we *know* is real because we can see it, hear it, taste it and touch it.

And we may think we're living in a world where the past has 'happened already' and is 'written in stone' and therefore immutable and unchangeable. The future is 'unknowable' because it is 'yet to happen' and we have to find ways of manipulating the present to arrive at that future.

That, in a nutshell, is our take on reality. But how do we know that's really right, or a true description of what is?

Well, let's talk a little about reality. Or at least how we perceive reality, and how our perceptions build up our map of reality ...

The first question you have to ask yourself is how do you know that you're alive and living in a world?

And how do you know that in this world there are other people, animals, places and lots of things going on 'out there'?

We know because of our senses. We can see it, hear it, feel it, taste it and smell it.

Everything that you experience, everything that you accept as 'real', everything that you take for granted as just being so, is the result of what you experience through your senses.

Our senses are something that we trust. We can't help but trust them in the normal, day-to-day running of our lives. We take our senses on faith, a faith so deep, so profound that for the most part, we don't even question it. It's that faith in what our senses are telling us that makes our physical lives possible.

The conventional explanation is that there is a 'physical world' full of stuff. That stuff is doing its thing, as stuff does. In the process of doing its thing, we are using our senses to detect it all.

The sense that we likely use the most is the sense of vision.

We open our eyes. We see stuff.

So let's talk about light.

Science tells us the following story of how it is that we see:

Physical matter is made up of very small 'particles' called protons, neutrons and electrons. These come together in various ways to form atoms and molecules. These atoms and molecules join up together in a bazillion arrangements to form the matter that we experience all around us, including the matter that makes up our own bodies.

Now, the thing about matter is that it's always moving around. Matter vibrates. It's hard to believe when you're looking at rock that it's moving much at all, but it is, in fact, incredibly active. All the matter that you experience in your day-to-day life is buzzing with energy and that energy expresses itself through vibration and radiation.

Radiation takes many forms, and one of the forms it takes is in other small 'particles' called photons. You can think of a photon as a wave of light traveling through space. We open our eyes. We see stuff, but what we are actually seeing are photons. Bazillions of them every second. Anything we see, we can see only because it is either producing light or reflecting light – because it is producing photons or reflecting them. You don't see anything until a photon or two, or several bazillion photons, are hitting your eyeball.

Take a moment to look at any light source. It could be a table lamp; it could be a ceiling light. If you're reading these words on an electronic device, the light is coming from a screen.

But if you're reading these words on a printed page, you're looking at reflected light. The paper itself is not producing any visible light. The only way that you can read these words on paper is if there is a light source that's emitting photons and if those photons are bouncing off the page and hitting your eyeball.

Simple.

Ah, but if only it were that simple. In fact, there's a lot going on that you're not consciously aware of, and it took scientists thousands of years to work it all out, and we're still working it out.

This is where things get a little more complicated.

For starters, even though all light is vibration, not all vibration is light, at least not as we understand it in our day-to-day lives.

The most powerful source of light in our general experience is that big ball of glowing plasma in the sky, the sun. The sun produces enormous amounts of energy. It really is a ridiculous amount of energy.

Every second the sun produces the same amount of energy as about one trillion atomic bombs, each of which would be exploding with the equivalent of a million tonnes of TNT. To put it another way, every second the sun produces more energy than the human race has ever used in all its history. In fact, every second it produces more energy than we would be using at our current levels of total energy consumption for 500,000 years. And it's producing all this energy in waves of photons.

Another interesting thing about our sun is that most of its radiation is in the form of light – visible light. But the words 'light' and 'radiation' mean roughly the same thing. But not all light is visible.

In case you hadn't noticed, the sun also produces a large amount of heat. But heat is just a different form of light, a different form of radiation. As I've said, radiation takes many different forms. One form is a photon. It's one form of electromagnetic (EM) radiation on the electromagnetic spectrum – the EMS.

The EMS is a range of energies in the form of waves, rippling out from a source, a bit like the way that waves spread out from the middle of a pond when you drop a stone into it. Waves have peaks, called crests, and valleys, called troughs. If you measure the length between peaks you get, you guessed it, a wavelength. Wavelength is an important thing to get a grasp on because it determines how you perceive and how you interpret radiation and EM energy. You experience this interpretation of EM radiation every day of your life without even thinking of it, because, in a way, your senses do all the interpreting for you.

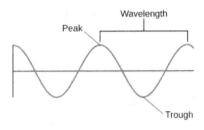

Let's take visible light. If you have color vision, you know that blue is a different color from red. But the difference you perceive isn't because blue light is 'blue colored' and red light is 'red colored'. 'Blue' and 'red' are simply the way that you perceive the same radiation at different wavelengths.

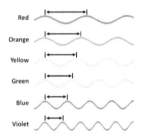

This brings me to my first major point:

The reality that you experience through your senses is an *interpreted* reality.

EM radiation is, in one sense, all the same thing, the same stuff. It's all the same energy 'stuff'. It's just your sense of sight that's turning different wavelengths of EM energy into different colors.

Color doesn't exist outside of your head. You are creating color, through your brain's interpretation of vibrational energy.

If you look at the spectrum of colors in a rainbow, you'll notice that the spectrum always follows a particular order – violet, dark blue (or indigo), light blue (or sky blue), green, yellow, orange, red.

In terms of wavelength, the shortest wavelengths are at the violet/blue end and the longest wavelengths are at the orange/red end. Every color you've ever seen is either one of these pure spectrum colors, or, much more likely, a blend of these colors in various mixtures and intensities.

Two 'colors' are worth a special mention. White isn't, strictly speaking, a color. 'White' is what happens when all the colors of the visible EMS hit your eyes at the same time. In reality this means that waves of violet all the way to red are coming at you all at once and your sense of vision says, "This is a bit full on! Oh, screw it, let's just call this 'white'," so that's what you see.

'Black', on the other hand, isn't strictly speaking a color either. Black is the absence of color. It's the absence of light. Black is what happens when there are no waves of photons of any type of visible light hitting your eyeball. Your sense of vision isn't getting anything it can register, so it says, "Oh, screw it. Let's just call this absence 'Black'."

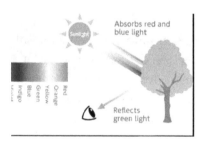

What's also worth noting is that any color an object appears to be is actually the exact opposite of what the color actually is. If you see a tree as green, for example, that's because the vibration you see as green is bouncing off of the tree and the tree is absorbing all the other colors. So in reality a tree is actually every color but green. That's true of course of everything you see. You are seeing an image as every color *except* the ones that it actually is.

The careful reader will note that I've been talking about *visible* light. But 'visible' light implies that there is such a thing as 'invisible light' and there's plenty of that around, but you can't see it, because, you guessed it, it's invisible! Or, at least, it's invisible to human eyes.

There are lots of ways that light can be 'invisible'. For starters, there are people, mostly men, who are color blind. Their eyes can't see particular colors because their eyes don't have the types of cells that are sensitive to particular wavelengths of light.

But even if you have all your eye cells in perfect working order and you have perfect color vision, there's still lots of invisible light out there that no human eye can see.

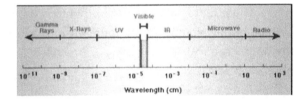

The visible light spectrum is only a VERY small part of the EMS. What wavelengths are shorter than violet? What wavelengths are longer than red? You're probably familiar with terms like ultraviolet and infrared, but most people don't think of these forms of radiation as light, even though that's exactly what they are. Ultraviolet or UV is simply a form of light that's 'beyond' violet, because that's what 'ultra' means in Latin. Infrared or IR is simply a form of light that's 'below' red, because 'infra' means 'below' in Latin. Latin isn't a dead language; science keeps on keeping it alive.

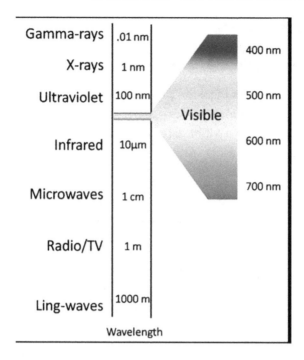

People often say that 'seeing is believing'. This is just another way of saying, 'I trust my sense of sight and if I can see it, I know it's there.' But ultraviolet light is 'real', as anyone who has ever had a sunburn can attest. At the other end, we also know infrared is 'real'; we just experience it as warmth.

This brings me to my next point:

Just because it's invisible doesn't mean it isn't there.

If you think of your body as a translation device, translating an 'external vibrational energy reality' into sensation, then understand that different parts of your body are designed to translate different types of vibrational energies into different sensations.

Your eyes translate visible light into colors. Your skin translates invisible light into tanning or warmth and will respond with burning if it gets too much of either type of energy.

Shorter wavelengths of light have higher energy, because a shorter wavelength can pack more energy into a given length. That makes higher energies potentially dangerous to your body.

Beyond ultraviolet there are X-rays and beyond X-rays there are gamma rays. Human senses cannot detect X-rays or gamma rays. They can do a lot of damage to your body because there's no sense that says move away now! This is unfortunate.

At the other end of the spectrum, below infrared, there are microwaves (yes, the same type of light that can heat your coffee) and below that, with ever-longer wavelengths, there are radio waves.

Gamma rays, X-rays, UV, infrared, microwaves and radio waves *were always there*, but until science started investigating the EMS, this reality was entirely invisible to humans.

Of course, that doesn't mean that these other lights were invisible to animals. Some insects can see ultraviolet and a flower looks very different to a honeybee than it does to us because flowers produce colors that are invisible to the human eye.

We have only four types of light-detecting cells in our eyes and we can only see three ultra-basic, primary colors – blue, yellow-green and red – from which all our other colors come. The mantis shrimp has 18 types of light-detecting cells in its eyes and can see 12 primary colors, which we don't have names for because nobody speaks mantis shrimp.

It wasn't until we realized that these many different energies were there in the first place, and we began to understand them, that we could build machines to see colors that other beings have been able to see for millions of years. It's only recently that we have had access to UV and infrared cameras.

And today we are literally bombarded day and night with Wi-Fi, 3G, 4G and 5G radiation and we can't see or feel any of it.

So when it comes to sight, we only see a tiny fraction of the light that's out there. We see colors when no color exists and even if color did exist, we see things as the opposite color to what they really are.

And yet we're so convinced that what we see is what's really out there. That we're seeing 'reality'.

Sound, taste, touch and hearing are very similar in that they are mostly just vibrations and we only perceive a very small percentage of what's really 'out there'.

But still we go through life trusting that what our senses are telling us is the 'truth', that it's 'reality'.

That 'sensing is believing'.

But is it?

Surely our senses don't lie to us.

Do they?

In fact, they lie to us all the time.

And as you'll 'see', this is just the tip of the iceberg when it comes to misperceiving our universe…

3

YOU'RE VIRTUALLY THERE!

WE LIVE IN A SCIENTIFIC AGE. Science is all around us. Even people who don't know much or care much about science benefit a lot from science and its practical application, technology.

Science works.

Science saves lives.

Science makes your life easier.

Science made this book possible, along with a whole bunch of other marvelous stuff that we take for granted. Stuff that our ancestors would have called 'miraculous' or 'magical'.

But science has its limitations and one of them is this:

Not all ideas are testable, and because they're not testable, they're also unprovable.

And one of the most untestable ideas is the idea of reality itself.

We've already established that your take on reality is, to a large extent, the result of information that you're getting through your senses.

Your senses are detectors of vibrations of energy. And, simply put, vibrations are just changes in energy that happen in quick, regular ways that we call waves – with peaks and troughs, with frequencies of different lengths.

Your senses work through the mechanism of nerve cells – specialized cells in your body that are sensitive to particular sorts of changes of particular types of energies. For example, the photoreceptor cells in your eyes are sensitive to changes in electromagnetic energy of a narrow range of very specific wavelengths we call the 'visible spectrum'.

And the same is true with our other senses. They all use nerve cells to communicate the information to your brain.

When we're touched, for example, that information travels electrically through our nerve cells to our brain, where our brain interprets the information as a touch.

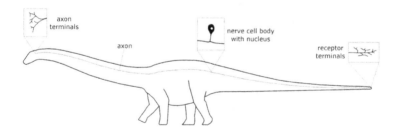

The important point is that the brain is only reacting to the electrical signal from the nerves. The brain is not actually seeing, hearing, tasting, touching and smelling. The brain is only interpreting electric signals.

Because there are so many steps in the chain of perception, the chain can be bent so that your perception of reality can become 'distorted' – hence optical, auditory, tactile and all sorts of other illusions.

This brings me to another extremely important point:

Your nerve cells don't even have to be exposed to the outside world vibrations that they're designed to detect in order to get activated.

Conduct this simple experiment on yourself.

Close your eyes, preferably in a dark room, and ever so gently and carefully press on your eyeballs.

All of a sudden, lights appear. In some people these might be very dim lights, in others they're brighter. These lights are called 'phosphenes'. Note that your eyes are closed, there's no chance for actual light to reach your eyes, but there are lights there anyway.

What you've done, in a very crude way, is you've activated the photoreceptor cells in your eyeballs with pressure to a point where they've said, "Well, I've been activated, time to send a signal to the brain, and since I'm a light cell, I'll say 'light'," and, in a matter of thousandths of a second, your brain has decided to say 'light', when all that your brain has received are electrical signals.

Remember that your brain lives in the dark. There's no light in your skull. The only reason that you 'see' light at all is because your brain has created it, in your head, based on electrical signals from your eyes.

It also works the other way round: your brain can construct a light image even when your eyes are closed and untouched by anything. This happens routinely when we dream. But you don't have to be asleep. When we're awake we sometimes call this capacity to create mind pictures 'imagination' – 'image nation' – in a sense, a whole 'nation' of images that exist because you've created them. This can happen with any sense.

The bottom line is that our entire experience of the world is completely dependent on what's going on *inside our heads*, not outside in the 'world'.

Our brain cells are called 'neurons'. There are neurons in charge of registering the experiences of each of our five material senses, and it's the activity of these neurons that creates our perceptions.

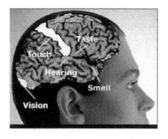

When someone touches your knee, for example, a signal travels from your knee, up your spine and into your brain. When that happens, the neurons in charge of feeling your knee are stimulated and that's when you experience the feeling of touch. But if those neurons are not stimulated, you don't feel it. If the signal gets blocked and never makes it to the brain, you feel nothing.

A perfect example of this is surgery. In surgery, someone could have their foot amputated and feel nothing, if they have the proper anesthesia. The anesthesia blocks the signal to the brain, so there's no sensation whatsoever. General anesthesia even blocks consciousness, so you don't remember the surgery.

But what's interesting is the flip side is also true. If someone were to go directly into your brain and stimulate the neurons in charge of inputs from your foot in the same way that they would have been stimulated during amputation, you would feel the sensation and all the horrible pain of having your foot amputated, even though no one is anywhere near your foot.

Sensation can be easily, *artificially*, constructed.

It's pretty incredible and scary to think about it, but you could experience the most horrible physical pain, simply by having those neurons stimulated in the right way.

In the Netflix series *Altered Carbon*, they did just that. In this dystopian world they had virtual interrogation/torture rooms where they would place a subject on a table and hook the brain up to electrodes. In an instant the person would be experiencing an interrogation/torture session, in their mind.

They'd still be on the table and NO ONE would be touching them. Yet they would see and feel themselves experiencing enormous pain and mutilation and it would all be fake. It would all be in their heads, just brain cells being stimulated in the right way. That's all. Their bodies would remain perfectly intact and untouched. But the pain would be just as real as 'real' pain and it would all be an illusion.

But this is also true of pleasure too. Let's look at sex. I think we can all agree that sex feels great, right? But if the signals to the brain are blocked, sex wouldn't feel like anything at all. If you have an epidural, for example, genitally focused sex would be meaningless. There would be no sensation from which to create an experience.

Conversely, if you stimulated the neurons in your brain that are in charge of sex, and you did it in the right way, you would feel all the amazing feelings of having sex, without your body being touched at all. I'm sure that there are people working on that as we speak!

And this is true of all of your five material senses. If you stimulated the correct neurons in your brain that are in charge of seeing a tree, you would see a tree. With the right technology you could smell the ocean or hear the wind or taste an amazing pie. All while you're lying on a table doing nothing. It's like your brain is a virtual reality computer that can have you experience anything simply by having your neurons stimulated the right way.

In fact, your entire experience of the world is completely dependent on how and when your neurons are being stimulated, and not at all based on what's actually going on in the 'real' world.

We take for granted that what we see, feel, taste, touch and smell is real and based on something really going on outside of ourselves, but there's no reason that has to be true.

With the proper technology you could stimulate all of the neurons in your brain to create an entire life experience that has no 'reality' behind it. And because the nervous system is chemical and electrical, we can accidently or, more intriguingly, deliberately, hijack the system using chemistry and electricity to create sensory and mental realities that seem completely 'real' to us, while having no correspondence in the 'real world'.

When scientists have an idea that they can't test, they sometimes come up with a 'thought experiment'. This is simply an experiment that exists as an idea or story that explores the logic of an idea or demonstrates a point.

One such thought experiment is 'The Brain in a Vat'.

Imagine a very advanced science that takes your brain out of your body and puts it in a vat filled with nice, warm, nourishing chemicals that keep your brain alive. Now hook up the brain to a computer that accurately duplicates the *exact* electrical signals that give you all the information from all your senses – sight, sound, smell, taste, touch – and even the senses that you don't normally think of as senses, but that nevertheless are senses, such as your sense of warmth or cold, your sense of up and down, sensations that tell you that you're moving, or swallowing, or digesting – the whole shebang. You'd be experiencing a completely artificial, virtual world.

And here's the big point.

You would not be able to distinguish a completely constructed and virtual reality from a 'real' reality.

How could you?

You wouldn't know that your brain was in a vat in some laboratory when everything else was telling you that you were, say, sitting in a room reading a book about how your brain is in a vat, which you'd think was ridiculous, because that's obviously not what you're experiencing.

Now take this experiment a step further to 'The Brain in the Hard Drive'. Imagine the science is even more advanced. Imagine that you could map the total of all the patterns of electrical signals that are passing through all of the cells in your brain. A pattern that totally recreated and simulated your experience of yourself.

Imagine that just the pattern was uploaded into a very sophisticated computer hard drive memory system that would make the world's most advanced computers of today look like a couple of scratches on a rock. It would have to be that sort of computer because even though there are about 100 billion neurons in each of our brains, they communicate through trillions of connections, called 'synapses'. The number of potential connections between all the neurons in our brains exceed the number of atoms in the known universe.

I'll say that again.

The number of potential connections between all the cells in your brain exceed the number of atoms in the known universe. You can literally create an entire universe in your head.

If you duplicated the pattern, the computer's circuits would take the place of your brain's neurons, and you would not need the messy 'wetware' in your head because it would have been replaced with software and hardware. Once again, you wouldn't be able to tell that this was the case because the beings that put you in this position could be manipulating every sensation, everything that was telling you what was real.

This would be true even if your 'thoughts' were your own. Our lives are already virtual, but a totally immersive, convincing and compelling sensory simulation would take virtuality to a whole new level.

And if this were the case, then none of us would be able to tell that we were living in a 'simulation'. None of us could know. We might all be living in a 'simulation', a completely constructed and artificial reality and we would never know, because any test that we could devise might just be part of the simulation.

Living in a simulation, whether in a vat or on a hard drive, would be like being in a very vivid dream and being unable to wake up, even if we suspected that we were in, fact, dreaming.

But how, within the simulation or the dream, could we devise a test that could 'prove' it, when the test itself might be just one more illusion?

Your brain in a vat could have the illusion of walking on the beach, making love, swimming, going to work, watching TV, and it would all be a total illusion and there would be no way to know. Movies like *The Matrix* and *Total Recall* are based on this undeniable fact. In both movies the brains of the characters have been hacked, like a computer, so that all of their life experiences are nothing more than just electrodes and chemistry interfacing with the brain.

Many modern-day philosophers and scientists have postulated that this world, this whole universe, is nothing more than a computer simulation. In the 17th Annual Isaac Asimov Panel Debate on April 5, 2016, Neil DeGrasse Tyson hosted a panel of thinkers who explored this at length. You can watch the YouTube video and read the transcript here:[1]

Nothing has to exist in the outside world in order for us to be having our life experience. It can all be just stimulation of our neurons and nothing more. The reality is the world could be nothing more than a creation of our minds and brains and there would be no way to know the difference.

It's simply IMPOSSIBLE to prove the world exists, based on the 'Big Five' of our material senses.

Here's a question for you: suppose someone in the next 20 years or so invents a virtual reality game that is so real it is *virtually* indistinguishable from 'reality'. Everything you experienced in the game looked, sounded, tasted, smelled and felt real, because it interacted with your brain in just the right way to make it all come to life.

Now let's imagine that in addition to being identical to a real-life experience, when you put on the headset to play the game, you also instantly forget who you really are. For the time you played the game, you had no recollection of your true identity whatsoever and actually believed, 100 percent, that you were your avatar in the game and living their life.

You might be a pirate, or an assassin or a pope or a martial arts master. The imaginary world you're living in might be peaceful or violent. It might be a utopia or a dystopia. Things might be easy or hard, but whatever the situation is, it's 100 percent real for you while you're playing the game.

The question is: would you play the game?

If the answer is yes (and sooner or later it would most likely be yes for everyone), you have to ask yourself, how do you know you're not playing that game right now?

Also, if you did choose to play this game, would you only choose lives and situations that were easy and enjoyable, like being a king or a movie star? Or would you sometimes pick some challenging experiences too?

Because in addition to having a good time in the game, you might also be able to use the technology as a way to test yourself and find out what you're made of. You might use this technology as an opportunity to learn and grow stronger, more disciplined, more loving, more patient.

It's in the situations that are hard or scary, the ones where life is not so easy, that you may be able to benefit the most.

In the 1990s hit sitcom *Seinfeld*, there's an episode where George is at a community center and there is a fire and he starts running over people and pushing them out of the way to get out of the building as fast as possible. He even steps over women with children to try to get out.

It was funny to watch, and George is a predictable character, when it comes to protecting his self-interest. But in watching the episode you can't help but ask yourself how you would react in that situation. Would we be the one to stop and help everyone out or would we pull a 'George'? Of course, we'd all like to think that we'd be a hero in that situation and many truly would be. But the only way we would know for sure how we would react is if we were in that situation ourselves.

Well, if we had this virtual reality machine, we could test ourselves and find out exactly how we would react. And if we didn't like the way we reacted maybe we could try it a number of times until we got better and better at reacting in the situation the way we wanted to. We could use the machine to become stronger, more courageous, more loving and accepting and become the person we'd like to be.

The point is: if such technology existed (and it very well could in the next 20 to 30 years), we'd most likely sooner or later play the game. We'd have the experience of being in a virtually real-life situation and completely forgetting our true identity while we played.

And, just as important, sooner or later, we'd probably choose challenging life situations to test ourselves, learn and grow.

We might even choose life situations that are EXACTLY like the ones we're experiencing right now!

If that's the case, you have to also ask yourself: are you playing that game right now?

It puts things into a whole new perspective when you consider the possibility that you may have actually chosen every aspect of your life for very specific reasons. Rather than being a victim of chance and circumstances, you might be the architect of your existence and you might have chosen all the events and situations to benefit you at some level. It's definitely food for thought.

So is the world real? Does it exist outside of our heads or is it nothing more than a creation of our brains and minds or some virtual reality game?

In order to answer this question, let's see what some of the greatest scientific minds of our time have to say about the 'real' world...

QUANTUM IMMORTALITY

4

ROCK SOLID EVIDENCE

ALL 'SOLID' objects in the universe are made up of atoms, as we've already mentioned. That includes our bodies, as well as all plants, animals and nonliving things. One way of visualizing an atom is like a tiny solar system, with a central 'sun' or nucleus, and electrons 'orbiting' around it. It's not really like that, but let's just go with this for now.

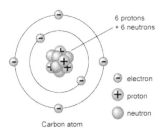

6 protons
+ 6 neutrons

⊖ electron

⊕ proton

◯ neutron

Carbon atom

So, in the same way, an atom has a nucleus at the center, which is like the sun in this example and it has electrons that orbit the nucleus.

The calcium atom looks like this:

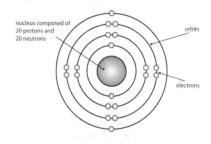

And here's the solar system:

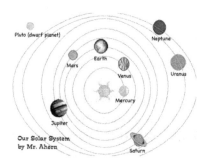

Think of how much space there is in our solar system. There's the sun, moon, planets, asteroids and a few other moons. Other than that, it's all empty space. In fact, our solar system is 99.999 percent empty space.

What's interesting about the atom is that, in spite of the diagram above, the relative space between the nucleus of the atom and the electrons 'orbiting it' is similar to the relative space of the sun and planets in our solar system.

That means that the atoms that make up our bodies and everything else, are also 99.999 percent empty space. We see ourselves and everyone and everything in the world as solid, when in reality we're all pretty much empty space.[1]

To get a better idea of what these scales are like: if an 'average' atom was the size of a football stadium, the nucleus would be the size of a marble in the middle of the 50-yard line, and the electrons would be flying around in a cloud in the seating area, and about the size of a grain of sand.[2]

I once heard a physicist say that if you remove all the empty space from all the atoms of the 7 billion people on this planet, we would all fit into a space about the size of a sugar cube – 7 billion people compacted into a sugar cube![3]

But even that isn't quite true. Electrons have about 1/1836 the mass of a proton and they're 'spread out' in a sort of cloud around the nucleus. We feel that a table is solid because of the action of the electron clouds of the table interacting with the electron clouds in our hands. But those clouds are not solid at all.

The only 'solid' parts of the atom are the particles that are inside the nucleus – and even that's questionable, because according to modern-day physicists, these particles are not solid at all; they are actually just waves of energy.[4]

Also, these waves of energy can exist inside an atom of our bodies and *anywhere else in the universe at the same time.* They can be inside our bodies, and on the other side of the universe and, very possibly, in any number of other universes ALL AT THE SAME TIME.

How did scientists come up with this stuff?

It sounds like gibberish.

And it would be gibberish, except that the gibberish that scientists have come up with is the reason that we live in a world today where we are surrounded by magical machines that actually work – miracles that we take for granted – things like TV, cell phones, computers, electricity – all based on the principles of quantum physics.

It's worth taking a little time to understand how we got here, and how the discoveries that got us here seem to indicate that there's an underlying reality that looks NOTHING like the reality we're used to, and that there are possibilities open to us that we have, as a society, barely begun to imagine.

This isn't a quantum physics textbook, so I promise to be gentle with you.

A Brief History of Quantum Physics

Quantum physics is the study of the tiny particles that make up atoms. The 'subatomic' particles, 'sub' meaning smaller, 'atomic' meaning atoms. The quantum world is the magical and mysterious world of subatomic particles.

The scientific knowledge we have of quantum physics is part of a tradition that goes back thousands of years.

The earliest record we have of ideas that ultimately led to quantum physics is in the surviving writings of the ancient Greek philosophers Leucippus, Democritus and Epicurus.

They asked a simple question: "If I cut something into ever smaller pieces, how small can I cut those pieces before I can't cut them anymore?" It was a question that took millennia to answer, but at least they gave us a word – atom – from *atomos* meaning 'uncuttable'. Other Greek philosophers were looking at the behavior of bigger stuff and developed a science of the way things move through space and how they behaved when you started poking around with things. This ultimately led to physics, which comes from the Greek words – *phusis* and *phusike* – which mean, respectively and approximately, 'nature' and 'the study of nature'.

Fast forward many centuries and alchemists were looking for the legendary 'philosopher's stone', a magical substance that could transform base, 'corruptible' metal into 'incorruptible' gold, and, as a side effect, grant immortality. Hundreds of years of mixing stuff up, heating and cooling things and lots of explosions later would lead to alchemy becoming chemistry and turning alchemists into chemists. As an interesting side note, the word for 'chemistry' as written in Chinese (and Japanese and Korean) translates as 'the study of metamorphosis'.

By the mid-1700s European 'natural philosophers' were making real progress into the nature of reality. By this time well-known geniuses such as Leonardo da Vinci and Isaac Newton, and lesser-known geniuses such as Giordano Bruno, had already asked, and in some cases answered, questions that would lead to the modern world. It was a long road, full of fits and starts and false leads, red herrings and reversals, but little by little some light was being cast on the darkness. By the end of that century, people like Antoine Lavoisier were getting closer and closer to a theory of matter that would make sense of everything.

Fast forward to today and we're left with some mind-blowing ideas about how subatomic particles behave, such as...

- **Quantum Tunneling**: A subatomic particle can go through 'solid' matter.[5]
- **Wave Particle Duality**: Photons and other bits of matter like electrons, protons and neutrons are both waves AND particles at the same time. Since all the matter that we're familiar with is made up of these 'wave particles', it follows that everything else, including you and me, are both particles and waves.[6]
- **Quantum Entanglement**: A 'particle' can be 'split' into two particles, each having half the energy of the original particle. To make a long story short again, if you then separate the particles and measure something called the 'spin' of one of the particles, the other particle always, and I mean ALWAYS, has the exact opposite spin. It's as if there is a communication between the two particles. The weird thing is that this 'communication' has been proven to travel faster than light. Einstein called this

'spooky action at a distance', since nothing is supposed to be able to travel faster than the speed of light.[7]

- **Quantum Superposition**: Subatomic particles can be in two places at once, and because bigger stuff is made up of subatomic particles it follows that bigger stuff can also be in two places at once. This was previously thought to be impossible. Scientists debated for decades that quantum phenomena were restricted to objects at the subatomic level, but in September 2019 the journal *Nature Physics* published the results of an experiment that showed a molecule made up of 2,000 atoms could be two places at once. It implies that, under the right circumstances, any collection of molecules – including you and me – could be in two places at once. Why this wasn't reported as the world-shattering news that it was is beyond me.[8]

- **Wave Probability Functions**: Theoretically an electron 'orbiting' the nucleus of an atom isn't in any particular place until it's interacted with or measured. Theoretically, that electron could be anywhere in the universe and is only actually 'there' (wherever 'there' is) when it's measured. It's only 'more likely' to be in the vicinity of the nucleus, but the probability that it's somewhere else isn't *impossible*, just *unlikely*. It follows that because 'everything' (including you and me) is made up of particles, you could theoretically be 'anywhere' – you're just more likely to be 'here' than 'there'.[9]

- **Uncertainty and Inherent Unpredictability**: There's no way of predicting where something 'will be' at the subatomic level.

- **Virtual Particles**: Things come into and out of existence for very brief periods of time from *absolutely nothing*. This is a result of something called a 'quantum field fluctuation'. There is speculation that the entire physical universe emerged from a quantum field fluctuation. This also conforms an Indian Vedic idea that the universe is in a constant state of fluctuating between creation and destruction, but that this is happening at a speed so fast that, to us, it seems like the universe is a continuing thing. It's the same as a movie made up of still frames, but because they flash in front of our eyes at 24 per second, our consciousness is just too slow to make out the frames individually, so they all blur together to give the illusion of continuous action and time 'passing'.[10]

- **The Multiverse**: That 'matter' and 'time' and 'space' might all be defined as 'wave functions' of infinite probability in a field of infinite universes that only 'decohere', or settle into one definite manifestation of reality, when you interact with that field. This is another theoretical basis for quantum computing, and we know that quantum computers have already been demonstrated to work, so there must be something to this idea (more on that in a little bit). In other words, there's an infinite number of universes that exist as potential universes and any one of them becomes 'real' once you interact with it.[11]

Individually, these quantum phenomena call into question what things actually are. Collectively, they form a picture that questions the very nature of existence itself.

We've already determined that the universe doesn't have to exist the way we 'see' it, in order for us to be having the experience of living our lives in a 'real', 'solid' world. Our brains are fully equipped to create the illusion of life, from start to finish, and there would be no way of us knowing that it was fake. It would be impossible to determine with our five material senses, or any number of other senses, alone.

So it turns out that even the so-called 'objective world' is just made up of empty space and 'probabilities', not 'actualities'. It seems that things don't exist until we, another set of probabilities, interact with them at some level, in some way.

I should point out that Einstein HATED quantum physics.[12] Things like quantum entanglement – 'spooky action at a distance' – seemed to violate the theory of relativity, that nothing could go faster than light. Furthermore, a world made up of inherently unpredictable uncertainty and probabilities is something that Einstein couldn't accept. He famously said that 'God does not play dice'. Quantum physics did Einstein's head in. This is deeply ironic, since it was Einstein's discoveries that did people's head in when he first proposed them. It's doubly ironic when you consider that it was Einstein's insights into the nature of time that ultimately led to the conclusion that time, in an absolute sense, doesn't exist either.

The Non-Existence of Time and of Everything Else

So we see ourselves as solid beings living in a solid world and it turns out we're all basically just empty space and waves of energy existing 'here' and anywhere else in the universe simultaneously.

And since we are just waves of energy all over the universe, let's look again at what those waves are. As we've said, a wave is measured by how fast it completes one cycle of moving from peak, to trough, to peak.

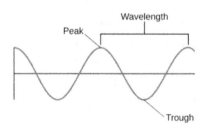

A wave is measured by 'cycles per second'. How many cycles a wave completes in a second is one of the ways we differentiate it from other waves.

But cycles per second are measured in time, and guess what? Time doesn't exist in an absolute sense. The most brilliant minds in the world tell us that time does not exist in a linear sense. No two events ever happen 'simultaneously' because the only way we know something has happened is when we interact with the consequences of it. If something happens on earth 'now', someone in a spaceship a light year's distance away won't know of the event for a year. The sun is eight-and-a-quarter light minutes' distance from earth. If the sun were to magically disappear right 'now', we wouldn't know about it for eight and a quarter minutes.

To all intents and purposes time is relativistic. Its 'passage' depends on where you are, or as physicists say, on your 'frame of reference'. And we KNOW that the 'passage of time' is affected by the rate of movement of an object and it's even affected by gravity.

This phenomenon is called 'time dilation'. If the satellites in orbit around the earth don't take gravity into account, the satellite navigation system that you rely on to tell you where your car is at any moment 'in time' goes out of sync by about 11 kilometers (about 5 miles) per day. At fast enough speeds, or in the vicinity of an immensely strong gravitational field, time stops altogether, or happens instantaneously, depending on your frame of reference.[13]

All time exists 'now' and we just perceive time to exist in one direction from past to future. But even that's not correct. Past, present and future exist in an eternal present and it's only our brain and senses that are telling us something different.

Time is relative, which is another way of saying it's not real in an objective sense. If you're moving at the speed of light, time completely stops. Now you might say that you're not moving at the speed of light, but there are lots of particles in the universe that are moving at the speed of light, including most of the particles that are in your body, so relative to them, you are not moving at all. Relative to them, the universe, for all its billions of years of existence, is happening 'simultaneously'.

In the 2014 movie *Interstellar*, Cooper, played by Matthew McConaughey, travels through a wormhole to a distant galaxy looking for habitable planets. Because he travels so far away, every hour that he spent there equates to seven years on earth.

He only spends about five or so hours over there and when he returns to this side of the wormhole, he watches videos of his daughter's entire childhood – her whole childhood gone in just a few hours. He missed the whole thing. It was both amazing and heartbreaking to watch.

But the math and physics are solid. If you travel far enough away and fast enough, every hour that you're alive could well be seven years or maybe even 1,000 years on earth.

So when you're measuring the particles that make up the universe in cycles per second and that 'second' could represent 1,000 years for you or even an eternity for you, depending on where you are or how fast you're moving relative to that particle, then nothing is 'really' moving at all. Time is not real and it's just our brains and minds that are making it all happen.

And when you look at two particles that are entangled – the communication between them is traveling faster than the speed of light – that means (according to Einstein) that the communication is traveling backwards in time. Then for you a communication cycle per second would not only be an eternity, it would happen in your past.

Either way, the most fundamental particles that make up the universe are not moving in a straight line through time. They're moving forward in time and moving backwards in time all simultaneously, depending on where you are relative to them.

We need time to define matter since there is no such thing as an 'instantaneous' thing. Something needs 'duration' in order to exist. So, if all we are is vibrations and vibrations are measured by time and time doesn't exist in an objective sense, then what really exists? If you need time to define matter, and time is not real in an absolute sense, then guess what? Neither is matter! It's that simple.

Just one electron in the whole universe?

And if time is instantaneous for a particle travelling at the speed of light, that particle is essentially ageless from our viewpoint or 'frame of reference'. And since time is irrelevant to that particle, there's no reason to believe that that particle can't travel 'backwards' in time either, as we just mentioned, because Einstein's relativity theory predicts that any particle travelling faster than light would travel backwards in time.

And if that's true, in theory there's no need to have more than one fundamental particle, endlessly traveling 'backward and forward' through time, to make up the entire universe of particles.

Because there's no reason to believe that this isn't happening, many of the greatest minds are also postulating that there may be only one fundamental particle in the entire universe! Currently this one particle hypothesis only applies to electrons. That is, some scientists have proposed that there may only be ONE electron in the entire universe, just moving backwards and forwards an infinite number of times to recreate itself and the illusion of many electrons.[14]

When an electron is moving forward in time it's an electron, and when it's moving backward in time it's something called a positron. But in theory there's no reason why this idea couldn't apply to any particle in the universe, since all those 'other' particles would simply be only other 'manifestations' of the one, fundamental particle anyway.

There are some holes in this theory. For example, there are more electrons in the universe than positrons. But what's amazing to me is that this idea is being taken seriously by some of the greatest minds on earth.

And other physicists are saying we live in a hologram or a movie. That the information of the universe exists in a two-dimensional plane, like a sheet of paper, and it's projected onto a screen to create the illusion of being three-dimensional.[15]

We know that quantum physics works. The computer I'm writing this on conforms to the predictions of quantum theory and is even limited in its functions to its predictions. We know that relativity works because it too makes accurate predictions about how things ought to behave, given our understanding.

The bottom line is that we see ourselves as solid beings, living in a solid world with other solid objects, going through time from past to future. But, in reality, we are just waves of energy, existing simultaneously all over this universe and perhaps an infinite number of other universes, traveling backwards and forwards in time-space in the eternal present. Also, we might just be a hologram AND it's possible that we're all just one particle! One single particle in the entire universe (or at least just one electron).

As mentioned previously, our brains have the ability to completely fabricate reality from nothing but electrical signals.

When we look outside our senses and use something as 'objective' as math and science to determine what's really 'out there', we can see that NOTHING REAL IS OUT THERE IN THE SO-CALLED 'REAL' WORLD.

We're left with the stunning conclusion that there is no 'objective' reality at all.

So what, then, are we experiencing?

Many modern-day physicists believe in the 'peekaboo' theory of the universe, which, as its name suggests, states that the universe is only real if we're 'peeking' at it. That is, the universe only exists if we're looking at it. Others suggest that the entire universe is one big neural network, like a giant brain.[16]

For all the logic or illogic of this argument, I can't say for certain if the universe is really 'peekaboo', although I'm inclined to think it is, based on my personal experience. As I've said before, the problem with testing reality is that reality itself, as a whole, is untestable, or at least we haven't worked out a way to test it. We can only test phenomena within reality to make some sort of conclusion, which in turn can produce a testable prediction.

But what I can say is true for sure is that the universe is certainly not what we think it is and certainly not what our brains are telling us it is.

And you can take this even further, because it's not just *this* universe that's fooling us; there might be *an infinite number of universes* that are fooling us into an experience of reality.

We might be living in an infinite number of universes simultaneously and not even know it.

5

FRANCIS JOSEPH COPENHAGEN AND THE DOUBLE-SLIT EXPERIMENT

PROBABLY THE MOST important experiment that has ever been conducted with respect to the nature of 'reality' is the double-slit experiment and its cousin, the Delayed Choice Experiment.

I want to talk about them briefly because they demonstrate how very 'spooky' reality really is...

In 1927 the infamous double-slit experiment forever changed the way we view the universe. Basically, the experiment shows us that if we're observing matter, it looks and acts like solid matter. But when we're not looking, it's not necessarily solid anymore; it can be and usually is a wave of energy, and in fact everything is usually a wave of energy, unless we're 'looking' at it. Only then does it act and behave like solid matter. This is true of tiny particles, like electrons and protons, and it's also true of atoms and molecules.[1]

In fact, matter will even go so far as to go back in time and change the past, in order to 'convince' you that it's solid, when you're looking at it, even though it's really just a wave of energy.

The way to understand the double-slit experiment is this...

Let's imagine you and I play a little game. I'm going to walk into a room. If you're not in the room I'm going to wear a red coat, but if you are in the room and you're looking at me, I'm going to wear a blue coat. Whenever you're not looking at me, I'm wearing a red coat, but as soon as you look, I put on my blue coat and as far as you know, my coat is always blue.

What's relevant about this experiment is the conclusions it makes about the nature of matter. And these conclusions are inescapable. Basically (and this is a VERY loose translation), all particles can act like waves of energy NOT solid matter unless we are looking at them. Yes, that's right! Unless we are looking at something it's just waves. The minute we look at it, it acts like a solid, but that ONLY happens when we are looking at it.

This includes small particles, like electrons and photons, but it also includes atoms and combinations of atoms called molecules. We're all made of atoms and molecules and those atoms and molecules are only acting like they are solid when we are observing them in some way.

And it goes even further…

The Delayed-Choice Experiment

Scientists devised an experiment that would force these small particles to commit to being either a wave of energy or solid matter BEFORE the scientists looked at the particles. Basically, if a particle commits to being a wave before being observed, it should stay a wave after it's observed. There's no going back. At least that's the way they designed the experiment. It can't turn into solid matter at that point. It's too late. And so in theory it has to remain a wave AFTER it's being observed.[2]

That's at least what should have happened. But that's not what happened. What actually happened blew everyone's socks off!

What they found and continue to find EVERY TIME they repeat this experiment is that if you look at a particle, even after it has already 'committed' to being a wave, it will still magically become a solid particle when you look at it, BECAUSE you looked at it.

In this experiment, in order for the particle to become solid matter once it's already committed to being a wave, the particle actually has to go BACK IN TIME to before it committed to being a wave and then 'recommit' to being a solid particle, based on your interaction, or 'observation' of it.

Let me repeat that – a wave of energy will go as far as to GO BACK IN TIME if has to, to become solid matter SIMPLY BECAUSE YOU LOOKED AT IT!

Using the same analogy we used before…

Let's imagine that I have to commit to wearing either a red coat or a blue coat before I walk into the room. I put on my red coat. Then, if you're not in the room looking at me, I keep on my red coat. If you are in the room looking at me, I go BACKWARDS IN TIME, leave the room, change my coat from red to blue and then walk in the room with a blue coat, as if I had always been wearing a blue coat.

Sounds pretty crazy, right?

According to this conclusion, WE ARE CREATING THE UNIVERSE WITH OUR MINDS and the universe is bending over backwards to accommodate us.

The waves of energy that make us up can go backwards in time, 'at will', and recreate the past, simply to satisfy our need to experience a 'real', 'solid' world in the 'present' anchored in a consistent 'past' and 'future'. And when that 'commitment' happens all the other 'states of potentiality' disappear or, in the parlance of quantum physics, 'the wave function collapses'.

This is called the 'Copenhagen Interpretation' of the double-slit experiment, named after the famous physicist Francis Joseph Copenhagen III...

Ok...

...I'm kidding about that...

...There's no Francis Copenhagen, it just sounded good. I'm pretty sure it's just named after the city, and the interpretation was largely devised by Niels Bohr and Werner Heisenberg in the 1920s :)

Anyway, the Copenhagen interpretation says that we, the 'observers', are collapsing the waves of energy into matter when we 'observe' them. We look at the wave and it becomes matter, even if it has to go backwards in time to do so. We're the ones doing it and we do it every time we observe the universe.

One of the biggest problems with this theory is it doesn't clearly define who and what an observer is. An 'observer' can be anyone or anything animate or inanimate and it still seems to work.

But there's another possible explanation: the many-worlds interpretation.

The many-worlds interpretation says that the wave is not collapsing. There are just two different worlds with two different versions of the particle that exist simultaneously. In one world the particle is a wave of energy and in the other world the particle is solid matter and when I observe the particle I'm simply observing the world where the particle is a solid.

So, the particle isn't going backwards in time, just to please me and I'm not mysteriously collapsing the wave into solid matter with the power of my mind (although I'm sure that's possible).

In this interpretation, when I look at the particle, I GO TO THE UNIVERSE WHERE THAT PARTICLE IS A SOLID.[3]

Using the same analogy above...

Let's imagine now that there are two different versions of me, in two parallel universes. In one universe I'm wearing my red coat and in the other universe I'm wearing my blue coat. I don't change them. Instead, YOU are the one making the change. You are moving back and forth between the two universes.

When you're not looking at me, you're in the universe where I'm wearing a red coat. When you're looking at me, YOU move to the universe where I'm wearing my blue coat. I don't change. I don't do anything. I'm just existing in both realities at the same time and YOU are moving back and forth between them.

The second explanation sounds crazy, but it would imply that there is more than one universe and that we are moving from universe to universe all the time without realizing it.

As crazy as the many-worlds explanation is, mathematically it makes more sense AND it's no longer just a theory...

The idea that there are an infinite number of parallel universes is not only being taken seriously, but Google and the U.S. Department of Defense have now spent hundreds of millions of dollars to build quantum computers that actually take advantage of parallel universes. These computers have the ability to do calculations in minutes that might take our best ordinary computers tens of thousands of years to perform.

In fact, in October 2019, Google's quantum computer solved a problem in 200 seconds that they say would have taken the best conventional computers over 10,000 years to solve. This is called 'quantum supremacy' and is the first example of this amazing phenomenon.

In December 2020, the Chinese Government's quantum computer solved a problem in a little under 3 1/2 minutes that would take the best conventional computers over 2 1/2 billion years to solve. To put that in perspective, if every single atom in this universe was a computer bit for a normal computer, the computer still couldn't solve the problem that fast![4]

The reason quantum computers are able to outperform conventional computers in such an outstanding fashion is that they can do their processing outside of time in an infinite number of parallel universes simultaneously. What happens is that the quantum particles access different versions of themselves in an infinite number of universes. They do the computations simultaneously outside of our timeline and then they come back to report the results.

Here's MIT physicist Max Tegmark talking about quantum computers and parallel universes in 2014…

There's a third kind of parallel universe

It's a discussion from studying not the biggest things but from studying the smallest things. By studying quantum mechanics, the rules that govern how it happens and how particles behave. This is arguably the most successful theory in all of science. It's given us transistors, computers, cell phones, lasers etc. but at the cost of some weird ideas, quantum mechanics tells [us]:

Little particles can be in several places at once. If the particles can be in several places at once, well, I'm made of these particles, I should be able to be in several places at once as well.

In 1957, a young graduate student named Hugh Everett worked this out really carefully and argued that what it really means is that there's a third kind of parallel universe where, when you make certain decisions, effectively our world splits into several parallel tracks. If I get a parking ticket, there's a parallel universe maybe where I didn't, but there's another parallel universe maybe where my car was stolen instead. You win some, you lose some.

This sounds very philosophical, but the way to test this, again, is not by speculating but by studying quantum mechanics more. Particularly, we should try to build quantum computers, which is a kind of machine which takes advantage of parallel computation effectively using these parallel worlds. If we try to build them, and there are millions and millions of dollars spent right now to try to do so, if it fails because we noticed that the basic equation of quantum mechanics is wrong, then we can forget about all of these parallel universes. But if they succeed and they can calculate something in five minutes that would take longer than the age of our universe to do on a normal computer, I think that will make many scientists take these parallel universes more seriously.[5]

That was back in 2014 before quantum computers were operational. Now they exist, they are in use and they're outperforming conventional computers...

David Deutsch, a physicist at the University of Oxford, says in his book *The Fabric of Reality* that quantum computers basically exploit parallel realities.[6] When you send the quantum computer a problem, it splits into multiple copies of itself in parallel realities. They all work on threads of their calculation, and they come back together again with the answer. He says the quantum computers are the first thing we've ever invented that takes advantage of parallel universes.[7]

So parallel universes exist and the biggest institutions in the world are now capitalizing on it. We're now using parallel universes to solve problems. The idea is no longer just a theory. It is part of the mechanics of our world.

And many physicists believe that 10 to the power of 500 other universes were created at the same time as ours...

In the late 1970s and early 1980s, several theorists began exploring what this relationship might mean on a cosmological scale. What they found in the math was that one trillionth of a trillionth of a trillionth of a second after the universe came into existence, space went through an "inflationary" stage that stretched its size a trillion-fold. What they also found in the math is that if the universe did arise out of a quantum pop – a nothing that became a something – that pop almost necessarily would have created other pops. And those other sudden somethings would, like the sudden something that became our universe, become other universes. The most common mathematical interpretation placed the number of such universes, before the self-replicating mechanism shut off, at 10^{500} – a one followed by 500 zeros.[8]

That's an inconceivably large number. A one with six zeros is a million. Every 3 more zeros is another set of numbers. A billion is a one with 9 zeros, a trillion is a one with 12 zeros and a quadrillion is a one with 15 zeros. This is FIVE HUNDRED zeroes! We don't even have a name for that number! To put it in perspective further, the number of atoms in the entire universe is only about 10^{82} or a 10 followed by 82 zeros. 10 to the 83rd power is ten times the number of atoms in this universe. This is 10 to the 500th power.[9]

So some of the top math minds in the world are predicting that at the time of creation a nearly infinite number of other universes were created at the same time. And now the biggest government and private organizations in the world are now capitalizing on these virtually infinite parallel universes.

Just as a side note, the idea that we're living in multiple parallel universes has been around in the mainstream consciousness for a long time.

According to Wikipedia there are 378 movies about time travel.

Some of the most famous time travel movies include: The *Back to the Future* movies, *The Terminator* series, Several *X-Men*, *Déjà Vu*,

Groundhog Day, Star Trek (2009), *Looper, Edge of Tomorrow, Harry Potter and the Prisoner of Azkaban, Bill and Ted's Excellent Adventure* and *Avengers: Endgame.*

ALERT – LOTS OF SPOILERS…

In *Back to the Future* Marty McFly's father was bullied as a kid and is now struggling financially. When Marty goes to the past and helps his father stand up to the bully he comes 'back to the present' and finds that his father is now a financial success. So there are two different, parallel universes, the one where his father is struggling and bullied and the one where his father finds his courage and is successful.

In *Groundhog Day* Bill Murray's character Phil repeats the same day hundreds of times, each time living in a separate reality – a separate universe.

In the movie *Déjà Vu*, agent Carlin, played by Denzel Washington, travels back in time a few days to stop a terrorist attack. So there's two different timelines. Two different universes. One where the attack happened and one where it didn't.

As soon as you introduce a new past – the one the characters travel back to and alter – you introduce a new universe.

In most of *The Terminator* movies the humans are able to stop the apocalypse from ever happening by killing the machines that travel back in time and then using their intel to stop the machines from ever becoming conscious and going to war with us in the first place.

But they didn't stop the apocalypse from happening. The apocalypse already happened, in *that timeline*. Once something happens it happens, you can't undo it, even if it's in the future relative to where you are in time. Because the future is happening now, just like the past and the present.

All they did was go to the universe where it never happened. When the machines and humans went back in time, they went to a parallel universe – a universe with a different timeline.

The universe where the apocalypse happened in 1996 didn't have terminators traveling back to 1984. The universe that had terminators traveling back to 1984 didn't have an apocalypse. Instead, what this universe had was terminators crossing over from the apocalypse universe to the peaceful one, which in effect stopped the apocalypse from happening in *this timeline*. Two different universes, two different timelines. It's a mindbender I know.

The way to think of it is this. Imagine a universe as a movie stretched out on the ground. The entire past, present and future, already created, already filmed and laid out in one long line of images.

Now imagine millions of other versions of this movie all stacked on top of each other. As soon as we travel forward or backward in time, we jump from one movie to another. Time isn't moving or changing and the story never changes, it's just us that's moving.

Time traveling is actually *timeline* traveling...

In *Terminator Genisys*, Kyle Reese was born in 2004 to a post apocalyptic world. From his very birth all he knew was war and struggle against the machines. In 2029 he travels back in time to 1984, helps stop the apocalypse and then travels to 2017 to try and stop it from occurring again.

The version of the world he travels to in 2017 never had an apocalypse. He meets the 13-year-old version of himself in this world and that version of himself is a normal kid, living a normal life, with parents, a house and a white picket fence. Two versions of the same person, living two totally different lives, in two totally different versions of the world – separate timelines in separate universes.

In *The Avenger Endgame*, they were very careful not to mess with different timelines. Thanos used the infinity stones to kill half of all life in the universe in 2018. In 2023 the avengers went back in time to before 2018 to get the stones and then bring everyone back. Their plan was to bring everyone back to 2023, not to reverse what happened in 2018. Then once they brought everyone back, their plan was to go back in time and replace each stone exactly where they found it at the exact moment they took it, so it wouldn't change the timeline at all.

In theory this could all be accomplished in one timeline. But a version of Thanos in 2014 figured out what they were doing and then travelled to 2023 to stop them. The version of Thanos that traveled to 2023 from 2014 isn't the same version of Thanos that killed everyone in 2018. Two different versions of Thanos from two different timelines exist in two different parallel universes.

In the midst of everything a 2014 version of Nebula meets herself in 2023 and kills the 2023 version of herself. Obviously the 2023 version of Nebula had a different history, otherwise she would have remembered meeting and killing herself when she was 9 years younger.

These were two different versions of Nebula, from two different realities – two different pasts existing in two different universes.

Also, once everyone was brought back to 2023, Steve Rogers (Captain America) went back in time to replace all the stones. After he replaced the stones, he decided to stay in the past with the love of his life and live the majority of the rest of his life with her. As soon as he did that, he created another timeline. Now there are two versions of Steve Rogers, one that is frozen for 70 years under ice and the other that's playing house with his sweetheart at the same time. Two different timelines, two different versions of the world, two different universes.

No matter how careful you are, you can't travel through time without creating multiple timelines in separate but parallel universes.

In Marvel's TV series *Agents of Shield* they had it all. In one season the main characters were trapped in a computer simulation, with no memory of their 'real' lives or their true identities. Just like we all could be right now, without realizing it.

In another season, they traveled 80 years into the future to see an existence in which the world had blown up and people were living like slaves on an alien station. When they went back to the present they were determined to prevent that future from happening.

Fitz, their chief quantum physicist said it was impossible to change the future. He said that time was an illusion and that the future, just like the present and past, had happened already. Since the future had already happened it was 'written in stone' and there was no way to change it.

Deek, who was Fitz's yet-to-be-born grandson, traveled back from the future with them. He explained to them that it was possible to change the future because we live in a multiverse of infinite parallel universes and you can change *your* future by traveling to an alternate version of the future.

They made a bet. If they changed the future it meant Deek was right and they were living in a multiverse. If not, Fitz was right and there was only one future that was written in stone. Of course they did change the future and Deek won the bet.

So, is time travel possible?

Who knows? But the particles that make up our bodies are traveling backwards and forwards through time continually and the only way they can do that is by using multiple universes.

Which leads us right back to Francis Joseph Copenhagen and what I call 'the Copenhagen paradox'. According to the Copenhagen interpretation, particles can go backwards in time to accommodate our expectations.

But the only way to travel through time is through multiple universes, as we just discussed. That means the Copenhagen interpretation also supports the many worlds theory and the idea of the existence of parallel universes.

So whether you believe in the Copenhagen interpretation or the many worlds idea, you can't escape the inevitability of parallel universes. Both ideas support the existence of a multiverse, despite the fact that they appear to be contrary at face value.

Both ideas point to the fact that the particles that make up our bodies are traveling from universe to universe all the time.

In the same way that the particles that exist 'inside' our bodies are moving through parallel universes all the time, we are most likely moving through parallel universes all the time and don't even realize it.

The many-worlds theory also gave birth to something called *quantum immortality.*

As we've touched on earlier, quantum immortality is the idea that every time we die in one world, there's a universe where there is a version of us that didn't die and our consciousness seamlessly moves from the world in which we died to the world in which we didn't die. This move is, to all intents and purposes, unconscious.[10]

For example, if you've ever had a close brush with death and somehow miraculously survived, it's possible that there were several versions of that story. In some versions you did die, in other versions you didn't die. If you're alive right now to tell about it, you're obviously in one of the versions where you didn't die. And in the versions where you died, your consciousness moved seamlessly to this life, so you can be here talking about what a close call you had and what a miracle it was that you survived.

This is a highly controversial theory. But I've often wondered how people manage to stay on this planet for 70, 80 or 90-plus years without dying of some freak accident. Well, according to quantum immortality, we don't. We probably die all the time; we just don't know it. We keep moving to the version of ourselves that dodged the bullet.

On September 11, 2001 I was almost on United Airlines Flight 93. That was the one that supposedly crashed in Pennsylvania. What really happened to the passengers on that flight remains a mystery. And when you do the research it's pretty chilling to hear some of the theories. But whatever happened to those people, it was only a fluke of fate that I wasn't one of them. I've always considered myself extremely lucky and I've often felt like the universe gave me a second chance.

But maybe the universe didn't just give me a second chance. Maybe I was one of those passengers too in another timeline. Both scary and comforting to think about.

Sometimes we don't even know we dodged the bullet, because we turned left instead of right and the disaster would have happened on the right. Or maybe when we're about to drive to work, we realize we forgot our phone, go back inside to get it and by doing so, avoid a car crash. Other times maybe we know we almost died and it becomes a story about how lucky we are or how someone 'up there' was looking out for us, such as my story.

This idea is completely untestable – you can't point to all the other dead 'yous' – but there is nothing about this idea that violates the laws of physics as we know them.

What I love about this idea is that it validates what I already know to be true from my own experience, which is that we're moving from universe to universe all the time, without knowing it. But, in my experience, this shift from one timeline to another doesn't just happen when we have a deadly accident; it's happening on a daily basis – moment by moment. It's part of our lives and we just don't realize it.

The same way a hot air balloon is moving higher and lower in the sky as it floats along, we're moving to higher and lower versions of ourselves all the time.

But it begs the question, if we are moving through universes all the time, what proof do we have?

6

MR. MANDELA AND THE MAGIC MIRROR

OK, we can see pretty clearly that the world's not what we think it is, and that it's not only possible that we're living in multiple universes, it's actually quite likely.

And we know that we could be moving through universes all the time and there would be no way for us to know, because the only way we experience life is through our physical senses and we know our senses lie to us all the time.

Our senses want to keep us alive, and safe and well fed and functioning and procreating and really don't give a stuff about how many universes we are existing in and moving through.

And I'm guessing that our senses, the little buggers that they are, know full well that if we had an awareness of all this it would blow our minds and make it very hard for us to function in the world and that would make it very hard for them to do their job well. So it's safe to assume that our senses, or at least that part of our consciousness that rules our physical senses, have a vested interest in keeping us from looking behind the curtain at what's REALLY going on.

Math and science are pointing to the fact that we're universe hoppers, even if our senses are hell bent on keeping that from us.

So the question is, if we were universe hoppers, what proof could we have in our everyday life? Well, the only thing that would be different for us if we moved from one universe to the other would be our memories of the 'past'…

Residual Proof of an Alternate Past

On May 6, 1937 the zeppelin known as the Hindenburg arrived in New Jersey after flying for three days over the Atlantic Ocean from Europe. The Hindenburg exploded as it was landing in New Jersey, killing 36 people.

It was a tragic event in history that will be remembered forever.

MORE SPOILER ALERTS

In the TV series *Timeless*, Lucy Preston was asked to travel back in time with a soldier and a pilot to track down a group of people who had stolen a time machine.

The people that had stolen this time machine used it to travel back in time to just before the Hindenburg explosion.

It turns out the people that stole the time machine wanted to prevent the Hindenburg from blowing up upon landing. Instead they wanted to blow it up on the way back to Europe, when several important US businessmen would be on board.

They were successful to some degree. They did prevent the Hindenburg from exploding upon landing and by doing so, changed the past. The Hindenburg did then explode on the way back to Europe but due to the intervention of Lucy and her team, only two people were killed.

When Lucy returned to the present day, she immediately noticed some changes. First of all, everyone who sent her on the mission now remembers the Hindenburg exploding on the way back to Europe, as it had done in this new timeline. No one remembered the original timeline version of the Hindenburg exploding while landing in New Jersey.

So Lucy and her team didn't go back to her original universe, she ended up in an alternate universe with a slightly different history.

When Lucy got home she discovered that her sister Amy had never been born in this timeline. But Lucy had a locket that she carried around her neck, back and forth through time. The locket went with her back in time to 1937 and then again back to the present in this altered timeline. The locket had a picture of her and Amy together. Proof that Amy once existed in another timeline.

That proof, is commonly referred to as "residual proof". And believe it or not, residual proof of alternate universes is all around us. If we look closely at our current lives, we may be able to find some pretty amazing residual proof of other lives, other timelines and other parallel universes…

The Mandela Effect

When Nelson Mandela died in 2013, I had this passing thought. It was, "I thought he was dead already." I remember him dying in the '90s in prison, and I remember a lawsuit between Winnie Mandela and his estate. I remember thinking, "What a shame that had to happen", because the whole lawsuit thing was really dragging his name, and his legacy, through the mud. But he didn't die then; he died in 2013.

I didn't think anything of it then, but later I learned that apparently there were millions of people who also had the same thought, so many that they give it a name. They called it 'the Mandela Effect', which is when a large group of people remember an event totally differently to how the event 'actually' occurred.

In effect, the Mandela Effect happens when people remember *different pasts.*

There are many examples of the Mandela Effect and when you see one that speaks to you personally it can be shocking. It can really rock your world. When you *know for certain* something happened in your past, and millions of other people remember it that way too, but it's apparently 'wrong', it can be pretty overwhelming, because you begin to question your sanity.

At the very least, you think that maybe you've just 'misremembered' something. At the worst, you think you might be going mad because the memory feels true and real and you'd swear on your grandmother's grave that the past you remembered actually happened. Except it didn't. Except that millions of other people also remember that past.

We know that human memory isn't perfect and it's 'reasonable and commonsensical' to assume that the Mandela Effect might be a case of 'mass misremembering'. But if quantum physics teaches us anything at all, it's that the 'reasonable and common sense' explanation isn't necessarily the *true* one. Quantum theory teaches us that if we're sincere about understanding reality, we might have to entertain ideas that don't conform to our current, demonstrably flawed perceptions and our assumptions based on those perceptions.

So, let's consider alternative explanations and whatever evidence we might have for them.

Many people believe that the Mandela Effect arises from the fact that we are moving through universes, with different timelines, at a very fast rate. Some have even pointed to CERN, the large particle accelerator in Switzerland, for the reason we're moving through universes so fast.

According to some people the work they're doing at CERN – at their Large Hadron Collider, with their constant experiments of smashing fundamental particles together at high energy – is causing little black holes that open up portals to other universes. Some argue that the particle physics that they're doing is a 'cover' and it's the opening of portals to other universes through black holes that's their real intention.

Some people believe these tiny black holes can annihilate our universe in an instant, and when that happens, we move to the next closest universe, without even realizing it – a kind of mass quantum immortality jump.

No less a physicist than Stephen Hawking remarked that CERN's activities could potentially annihilate our universe in a matter of seconds. The black holes that they are creating would have to be bigger, by his calculations, but once they were, we'd be toast.

And maybe they've done it many times already and we *were* toast. Maybe it's happening all the time and we don't realize it because we just keep moving to the next 'available' universe each time, with all of our collective consciousness blithely intact.

And, of course, neither the Mandela Effect nor a black hole conspiracy theory of CERN's 'real' agenda is proof positive that we are moving through universes. There are lots of psychological theories that try to explain the Mandela Effect that have nothing to do with us moving through worlds. But none of these psychological theories are based on any type of substantial evidence either. Some I find highly condescending and dismissive too. It's arrogant to be so condescending about something that is so impossible to prove and have virtually NO shred of evidence supporting it. It's simply not something that can be proved or disproved, so we're free to speculate, and to go where that speculation might take us.

Nevertheless, in light of everything we've been talking about in this book, and the high likelihood that parallel universes are now a part of our everyday life, it's worth investigating the possibility that this phenomenon may very well be examples of 'universe hopping'.

There are several Mandela Effects that speak to me personally. I'll mention a few of them briefly here. But if you're interested, I would encourage you to do some research on the internet. There are lots of videos on YouTube with some great examples.

But let's look at few here:

The Lion and the Lamb

Biblical Mandela Effects are great because there are a lot of people out there who REALLY know their Bible and can assert with a high degree of certainty that 'something' has changed. The biggest biblical Mandela Effect is 'The Lion and the Lamb'.

The question comes down to a biblical prophecy, a verse, Isaiah 11:6. People remember this as 'And the lion shall lie down with the lamb'. If you ask any group familiar with the Bible at random, "What shall lie down with the lamb?" they'll almost universally answer, 'the lion'. But the answer is actually, 'the wolf'.

The wolf shall dwell with the lamb,

and the leopard shall lie down with the young goat,

and the calf and the lion and the fattened calf together;

and a little child shall lead them.

— ISAIAH 11:6

Again and again even 'experts' assert that it's 'lion', but it isn't. These experts are biblical scholars, Christian pastors and even rabbis and students of the Torah, and the 'mistake' crops up all the time.

In one video a rabbi is showing the passage in his Bible and he says "The lion shall lie down with the lamb"[1]

Here's an expert talking about it....

Biblical Scholar: ...I studied under Dr. Gene Scott for almost 30 years and have carried on his message an additional eight years. I base my scholarship on Dr. Scott's scholarship and teaching, as well as on my own research and studying that I've done independently...

...In Isaiah 11, most everybody's familiar with that saying. You may not know it as Isaiah 11, but the question is what shall lay down with the lamb?

Answer in the audience: The lion.

At home, answer out loud.

Lion.

The lion shall lay down with the lamb etc. Now in this reality, it says, "The wolf shall lay down with the lamb.

Again, like I said before, check it out."

In another video, a lady is calling a biblical scholar...[2]

Woman: Oh, great. Awesome. I have some questions. I'm a believer and I just had a question. Do you remember that scripture from Isaiah 11:6 by heart about a certain animal shall lay with the lamb?

Expert: A lion shall lay down with a lamb. Is that what you're talking about?

Woman: Okay, yeah. Yeah, that one. Have you actually read that one? Do you remember actually reading it for yourself with your own eyes in Isaiah 11:6?

Expert: Mm-hmm (affirmative). Yeah.

Woman: Okay, yeah. That's what I always thought because the lion represented Jesus, the lion and the tribe of Jews, and the lion was us, the saints. What's really odd is that my bible doesn't say lion. No bible says lion anymore. It says wolf. Did you know that?

Expert: Well, I mean ... Okay. Hang on just one second. Let me go get my bible. Okay?

Expert: Okay. This is in the revised version. "The wolf also shall dwell with the lamb, and the leopard shall lie down with the kid; and the calf and the lion and the fatling together; and a little child shall lead them. And the cow and the bear shall feed; their young ones shall lie down together: and the lion shall eat straw like the ox." All right...

Then there's a jeopardy clip on YouTube on this subject:[3]

Nan: Proverbs 600.

Alex Trebeck: "The lion shall lie down with" this animal.

Alex Trebeck: Mary Grace?

Mary Grace: What is the lamb?

Alex Trebeck: Correct.

How does that happen?

I remember when Woody Allen wrote the book *Without Feathers*. I was 10 years old. I loved that book. It was very funny. He said, "The lion shall lay down with the lamb, but the lamb won't get much rest."

Now it *may be* that it's just a common misconception that we think the saying is "the lion shall lay down with the lamb" when it's actually the wolf. And I would believe that except for the fact that so many *experts* remember it being lion as well.

The Fairest One of All

Here's another one of my favorites. How did the wicked queen in *Snow White* determine "who is the fairest one of all?" What question did she ask the mirror?

"Something, something on the wall, who is the fairest one of all?"

Most of us remember it as "Mirror, Mirror" on the wall, but it's actually *"Magic Mirror"* on the wall.[4]

Magic Mirror?

Really?

I'm sure there's millions of people that remember it as 'magic mirror' but I personally don't know a SINGLE person who remembers it that way. Even in the latest reimagining of *Snow White* called *Maleficent*, Charlize Theron, playing the queen says, "Mirror, Mirror on the wall". Why would she say that if it's "Magic Mirror"? Are we *all* just misremembering?

Maybe it always was, and people only think "Mirror, Mirror" because they haven't seen, or have forgotten, the Disney movie. I don't know. What do you think?

We Are the Champions

Speaking of other queens…

We all know the Queen song 'We are the Champions'.

How does it end? Many of us remember it ending like this:

"We are the champions.

No time for losers 'cause we are the champions…

[pause for effect] …

Of the world."

But apparently that's not how it ends. It just ends at "we are the champions" without that final "of the world".

There's an entertaining clip of James Corden in carpool karaoke. He's with Gwen Stefani, George Clooney and Julia Roberts. Their singing 'We are the Champions' and waiting for the bit at the end. They seemed confused and cheated when it didn't come...[5]

Gwen Stefani: What?

James Corden: You don't do another "of the world"!

Julia Roberts: Oh my god!

James Corden: I always thought you did another "of the world"!

Gwen Stefani: That's crazy!

George Clooney: They really should have. That's really rough, man.

Gwen Stefani: We were like ... waiting.

James Corden: We were all in the zone though, guys.

Gwen Stefani: We were loaded. It was like the gun was loaded and ready to shoot.

James Corden: I could feel it going through us though, wasn't it?

This is the actual moment when the song has just finished and they are waiting for the 'of the world'...[6]

Scarecrow's Gun

Did you know the scarecrow in *The Wizard of Oz* had a gun? You can watch a clip of him holding his six-shooter here:[7]

There he is, ready to shoot.

This one makes no sense to me because no one in the movie had a gun. And if he did have a gun why should he be scared of the Witch, the flying monkeys, the Wizard or anyone else. He was the only one packing! Maybe he was scared to use it?

The point is: *nobody* remembers the gun.

The Curious Case of Ed McMahon and the Checks

Best remembered, accurately, as Johnny Carson's sidekick, Americans remember Ed McMahon delivering prize-winning checks from a company called Publishers Clearing House, who give away prize money in sweepstakes as a promotion for their brand.

Do you remember Ed McMahon going to people's houses delivering big checks for Publishers Clearing House? Apparently, lots of people do. Lots of people remember this going on *for years*.

Well, apparently, Ed *never* went to people's houses delivering checks and he *never* worked for Publishers Clearing House. He worked for another company I never heard of called American Family Publishers. He made some commercials for them, but he never delivered checks.

There's an article in *Forbes* magazine about it:

"Ed McMahon never worked for Publishers Clearing House. He was a spokesman for American Family Publishers. McMahon never left the studio to ambush families, and he never held a giant check.

Similarly, Publishers Clearing House never hired a celebrity to serve as a spokesperson, and it was the Prize Patrol, not McMahon, that showed up on doorsteps with a giant check."[8]

Here's the thing that doesn't make sense about that. In interviews and even other commercials Ed McMahon recalled delivering checks and he talked about delivering checks door to door.

There's a hilarious rap song Ed does in a commercial, where he's talking about how he used to deliver checks...[9]

This song goes like this...

Ed McMahon: Shout out to my people. This is Ed McMahon rolling slow through the suburbs in an unmarked van. I ran the strip in the '80s, brought big fat checks to the ladies. When I showed up at their door, ladies start screaming like crazy. Raking it in hand over fist. Was on the VIP list. I was a verbal gunslinger and my shots never miss but now the bills have come due and my credit score's wacked, so I'm hitting up the winners to get my checks back.

Ed McMahon (going door to door talking to previous winners) Do you remember I gave you that big check? I'd like to have that check back. I'm having some ... That would help a lot. Just a little bit.

Here's a commercial where he's talking about Neighborhood Watch. He goes to a lady's door to talk with her and she goes absolutely crazy, thinking Ed is bringing her a check:[10]

Ed McMahon: Mrs. Bruzzo, I'm here with the Neighborhood Watch.

Mrs. Bruzzo: You're Ed McMahon? Yes! (screams like crazy)

Ed McMahon: Yep.

Mrs. Bruzzo: Ah!

Ed McMahon: I'm with Neighborhood Watch.

Mrs. Bruzzo: You made our dreams come true! Ed McMahon is here. We're going to be rich!!! It's Ed Mcmohan.

Ed McMahon, leaving: I'm going to check with the lady next door.

And there's a clip of Ed appearing on the *Roseanne* show delivering a huge check to Roseanne...[11]

Roseanne Barr: Who are you supposed to be?

Ed McMahon: Well, hi. I'm Ed McMahon. You won our special Halloween jackpot.

Roseanne Barr: Okay. What is a refrigerator, a pool-side dressing room, and Ed McMahon?

Ed McMahon: A refrigerator, a pool-side dressing room, Ed McMahon.

Roseanne Barr: What is a Havana, a cabana, and a famous second banana?

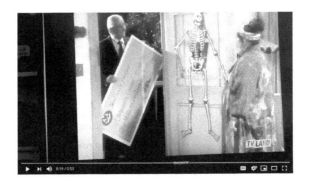

Johnny Carson, who worked side by side with Ed for over 30 years, remembers him working for Publishers Clearing House and delivering huge checks.[12] In this video Johnny is delivering a giant check to David Letterman...[13]

David Letterman: Nice to see you.

Johnny Carson: I have to apologize. I thought this was the Joe Franklin studio. I'll tell you why I'm here. I happen to be in town. We're doing some stuff with an NBC affiliate.

David Letterman: That's right.

Johnny Carson: Ed McMahon, our good friend, could not be here, but it seems, David, that you are the $1 million winner.

David Letterman: Oh my god! I won a million!

If you look at the check in this video, it says 'Publishers Clearing House' on it. You would think that Johnny Carson would know if Ed McMahon worked for PCH or not. It's one thing for you or me to mix that up, but Johnny and his writers? That doesn't make too much sense.

Nevertheless, Publishers Clearing House is a real company. Its sweepstakes are real and so are their checks. So who gives out the checks in 'real life', especially since Ed McMahon died in 2009 (at least in this reality)?

Apparently, it was The Publishers Clearing House Prize Patrol.

I never heard of them. And look at how small the checks are…

… these checks look like postage stamps compared to the big checks *I* remember Ed McMahon delivering. *I have completely different memories of these events and so do millions of other people.*

And here's a couple other common 'Mandelas'.

Dorian Gray

The Picture of Dorian Gray is a novel by Oscar Wilde.

Many people remember the book being called *The Portrait of Dorian Gray*.

You can even find *The Portrait of Dorian Gray* for sale online.[14]

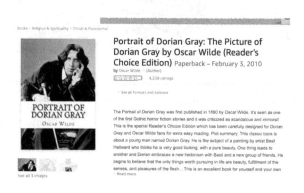

In this instance it says *Portrait of Dorian Gray: The Picture of Dorian Gray*. Why would it say both" Apparently it has always been 'Picture'.

In the Marilyn Monroe movie *The Seven Year Itch*, they talk about the book and refer to it as *"The Portrait of Dorian Grey"*.[15]

"I've been thinking about that fall list. And I came up with a little ... What would you think about a 25-cent reprint of The Portrait of Dorian Gray?"

"The Portrait of Dorian Gray?"

"It's a natural! Look what we'll be giving them for a quarter!"

And there's also a lady on YouTube giving a review of her favorite books. Keep in mind, this is one of her *favorite* books, *The "Portrait" of Dorian Gray*.[16]

"Oscar Wilde and Bram Stoker. These guys are a duo of Gothic wonderment. Dracula *is the big daddy of vampire stories. You know the drill: don't go out in Transylvania after dark. And* The Portrait of Dorian Gray, *that story of a narcissist...."*

She's calling it "The Portrait of Dorian Gray".

She's *read* it.

It's one of her *favorite* books.

She's doing a *review* on it.

She's **holding the book** with the title on it.

The title actually says, "The Picture of Dorian Gray".

She's got the name of the book wrong and it's supposedly one of her *favorite* books.

How does that happen?

The Italian, Spanish and Chinese translations of the book use "The Portrait", not "Picture" and most of all, the book is actually about a *portrait* of Dorian Gray, not a picture of him.

Here's a few others...

- **Bruce Springsteen,** *Born to Run* **album cover** – many people remember him having a red bandana in his back pocket. Now he has a red hat.

- **Berenstain Bears** – many remember this childhood bear being spelled "Berestein bears". This makes sense as Berenstein is the common spelling of this name, but it's still "Berenstain".
- **The JFK assassination** – the car JFK was assassinated had six people in it, but many remember it being only four people. A model of the car in the Henry Ford Museum is of a 1961 Standard Lincoln *four-seater*.
- **The Smithsonian Institution**. Many of us remember the Smithsonian being called "The Smithsonian Institute". But it's never been called that; apparently it has always been "The Smithsonian Institution".
- **Grand Central Terminal**. Apparently "Grand Central Station" in New York City has always been "Grand Central Terminal", not "Grand Central Station". I lived next door to it *for seven years* and never heard *anyone* call it "Grand Central Terminal". Maybe that's just one of those examples where everyone just called it station and the name just stuck. Who knows? But I was pretty surprised to hear about this.
- **Haas avocados**. Did you have Haas avocados when you were young? Many of us don't remember them being around until the 2000s. The first time I saw one was in 2007 in Australia and I just assumed it was an Australian version and that's why it was new to me. But apparently they've always been around. Do you remember them when you were a kid?
- **Looney Tunes** – most people remember "tunes" being spelled "toons". This makes sense because "toons" is short for "cartoons". "Tunes" typically refer to a song, like iTunes. Not only are they cartoons and not songs, but the abbreviation for a song being a "tune" probably

originated in the 70s or 80s. Looney Tunes have been around since at least the 50s.

They never said it.

These famous lines were apparently never said in this timeline:

'Beam me up, Scottie' (Captain Kirk of *Star Trek*)

'Me Tarzan, you Jane' (Tarzan obviously)

'Lucy, you have some splanin to do' (*I Love Lucy*)

I personally remember hearing all of these iconic phrases on several occasions.

- **'It's a beautiful day in *this* neighborhood.'**

Most people remember the words of Mr. Rogers' theme song to be, "It's a beautiful day in *the* neighborhood" not "this" neighborhood. It makes sense that it would be "the" and not "this" as Mr. Rogers would likely want to include all the children watching, which "the neighborhood" does and "this" does not. Also, Tom Hanks stars in a 2019 film about the life of Mr. Rogers called *A Beautiful Day in* the *Neighborhood*. How could you make a film about a celebrity and get the name of his theme song wrong in the very title of the movie? It doesn't make too much sense.

- **'*You're* gonna need a bigger boat.'**

In the movie *Jaws*, I distinctly remember Sheriff Brody saying, "We're gonna need a bigger boat", and so do millions of other people. It makes sense that he would say "We're gonna need a bigger boat" and not "You're gonna need a bigger boat" because he was on the boat too.

- **"Luke, I am your father"**

Is that the way you remember that famous line from *Star Wars*? Most people remember the line that way. Apparently, Darth Vader never said that; he said, "No, I am your father". This seems like a small difference but both James Earl Jones (the voice of Darth Vader) and Mark Hamill (Luke Skywalker) remember the line as "Luke, I am your father".

In a video clip on YouTube James Earl Jones is talking about his reactions when he first heard the line and he says, "When I first heard the line "Luke, I am your father," I said to myself 'He's lying. I wonder how they're going to play that lie out'."[17]

In another video clip at 4:11 Mark Hamill is pranking an actor who is playing the part of Darth Vader for an audition. He's right behind the actor, when the actor says the line "Luke, I am your father". Earlier Hamill refers to the line as one of the iconic *Star Wars* lines.[18]

So it seems like a small thing, but millions of people remember it as "Luke, I am your father", and the only two people that were in the actual scene remember it that way too, so it can't easily be dismissed.

Continuing the theme of *Star Wars* for a second, in this timeline, Darth has a silver nose and C-3PO has a silver leg. Most people remember Darth Vader's mask as all black and C-3PO's body as all gold.

Here's a picture of Darth in his current silver nose job form....

Yet a quick search on Google Images reveals hundreds of images of Darth with a black nose. Most toy masks have a black nose too.

Here's a clip of the original scene where Darth is telling Luke he is Luke's father. In this scene his nose is clearly black...[19]

It may just be lighting or some other explanation. Who knows?

Then there's …

Mona Lisa's smile

All of us know about Leonardo da Vinci's world-famous work of art, the *Mona Lisa*, the other name of which is *La Gioconda*. The secret of Mona Lisa's smile has intrigued humankind for decades. Many people have claimed that Mona Lisa's actual portrait never had her smiling. They say that the lady in the portrait had a hardly detectable smile, more like an expression of boredom. However, in reality, Mona Lisa's smile is pretty obvious, almost bordering a smirk, but that is not how a large majority of people remember her.[20]

Here is how one art student remembers the smile:[21]

How I remembered the Mona Lisa

Hi, I'm a professional graphic designer and I stumbled on the Mandela effect and thought it was interesting. While I attributed most of them to false memory, I came across the Mona Lisa where someone claimed "Mona Lisa never had a smile or smirk". I thought to myself, that's right she never did.

So I went straight to Google Images and searched "The Mona Lisa". The first picture showed up, which was in Wikipedia, I clicked on it to get a full-sized view and the hairs on my arm stood up. It seriously looked like someone went into Photoshop and modified her face to make her smile/smirk. It just doesn't look like how I remembered it, also I'd never even seen her with a veil on. The Mona Lisa really fascinated me before and I would watch lots of documentaries on it.

She was always depicted as a mysterious person to the point they wonder if it was a self-portrait of Leonardo da Vinci himself. To me she always had a blank, unexpressive and enigmatic face. No smile! In fact the one I see smirking now gives me the creeps! Ha ha.

So I downloaded the photo and got to work to try and depict how I remembered her.

1. *First off I never remember her wearing a veil so I Photoshopped it off.*
2. *Then I had to get rid of her smirk, I had to first adjust it just enough to where she's no longer smirking, then get rid of the indentations on the side of her lips caused by her smirk.*

What's weird is that the area around her mouth is very smooth, almost as if it was airbrushed compared to the rest of her face which depicts artwork aging. It looks very strange so I added the same old texture that's on her forehead to her mouth region.

And on the below link is what I came up with.[22] *On the left side is the real Mona Lisa, on the right side is my rendition. This maybe is just all of us having some false memory, but I cannot get this one out of my head, especially for someone who **studied** the Mona Lisa and loves art.*

The Lindbergh Baby

In March of 1932 famous aviator Charles Lindbergh's baby was kidnapped. Many of us remember that it remained an unsolved mystery. I even have a friend who is a relative of Charles Lindberg and we've talked about it many times.

My memory is that the baby was never found, and it remained forever a mystery as to what happened to him. I was born 32 years after this event and it was still a hot topic when I was a kid.

But the *actual* version in the timeline in which I currently find myself is that the baby was found dead, tragically, three months later and the kidnapper was found just after that. Case solved, no mystery.

The thing that doesn't make much sense about this is that if the baby was found, why was it still something people were talking about 50 years later? It would have been just another tragic event in our history. Also many of us remember his name was spelled Lindburgh.

The Japanese Bombing of the Continental United States

Did you know that the Japanese bombed the continental U.S. 300 times during WW2?

I didn't.

In fact, they sent over 9500 'balloon bombs' also known as FU GO bombs or "fire balloons", over the Pacific toward the United States in 1944–45. Some 300 of them made it to U.S. soil and killed six people. I didn't know that, and I never heard of any such thing in my history classes. I would think it would be a really big deal that U.S. citizens had been killed by Japanese bombs on U.S. soil. Think of how big a deal Pearl Harbor was. Have you heard of this? No one I've *ever* spoken to has any recollection of this 'fact'.[23]

The Thinker

Rodin's famous 'Thinking Man' statue.

This is the correct version in this timeline:

This is the way many people remember it:

Which one do you remember? I remember the version where his hand is on his forehead. But that's not the correct version. The 'correct' version has his hand on his chin.

Did the Grinch Steal Christmas?

Growing up I always knew this story as *The Grinch Who Stole Christmas*. But it's actually *How The Grinch Stole Christmas*. Which do *you* remember?

I have friends who remember it both ways. What's interesting is that there's no right or wrong answer. Both realities exist, at the very least in people's minds, but what I'm arguing is that what you remember depends on which timeline you grew up in.

Remember that as you're going through these examples. They don't have to all be 'right' to you. We all are moving through universes according to our own experiences.

The Salem Witch Trials

In school I learned that 'witches' were burned at the stake during the Salem Witch Trials. The way it was taught to me was that they were plunged into water. If they died it meant they were innocent. If they lived it meant they were witches and would be burned at the stake. Without question one of the darkest spots in our history. But that's not exactly how it goes in the reality I currently find myself in.

In this reality they were hanged, not burned. Still horrific nonetheless, just not what I remember.

Fruit of the Loom's Cornucopia

There's a big American brand of underwear called Fruit of the Loom. Do you remember its logo? Many remember the logo as featuring a 'Horn of Plenty', or cornucopia.

So, does it have a cornucopia or not?

I distinctly remember the logo having a cornucopia.

Now it's just fruit.

Most people remember the logo looking like this:[24]

But this is the actual logo…[25]

Here's an article where a model for Fruit of the Loom talks about how the logo used to have a cornucopia...[26]

Underwear character is still a-peeling

ET TU, FRUI-TAY?: Of the many surprises we menfolk discover in our underwear every now and then, fruit is among the rarest. The last time underwear fruit happened to me, it was a ripe mango. But that was years ago, during Richard Nixon . . .

BILLY COX

PEOPLE

Anyhow (aside from bananas), fruit images and underwear rarely grow on the same vine. And even today, Sam Wright looks back on that aspect of his career with bewilderment. The corporation never fully explained the concept to him, even though he played purple grapes.

Wright comes to Melbourne Sunday for Kids Jam USA, a live family-entertainment gig at Brevard Community College's King Center. For this incarnation, Wright will assume the Sebastian The Crab persona he cultivated in the Disney film, "The Little Mermaid."

But for 19 years, Wright made anywhere from 120-140 television commercials for Fruit of the Loom underwear. And he didn't even wear Fruit of the Looms. He wore skimpy bikini briefs. "My wife is European," he says from a hotel room in Tampa. "She said (cotton underwear) made me look like an old man."

Anyhow, Fruit of the Loom's logo was initially a cornucopia swollen with an apple, green grapes, purple grapes, and their green leaves. Wright was the purple grape cluster. And he had to pretend Fruit of the Looms ("I never found them that comfortable") were great.

"Our job was to get more people excited about wearing Fruit of the Loom," Wright says. "As fruit, we knew the waistband was stretchable, because we lived there."

Cornucopia of job cuts

Fruit of the Loom Inc. said it would slash its U.S. work force by 12 percent by eliminating 3,200 jobs in five Southern states by year-end to improve profitability. Six plants will be closed and operations will be reduced at two others. The nation's largest underwear maker said the affected plants were in Kentucky, North Carolina, Mississippi, Alabama and Louisiana.

The firm's profits dropped 39 percent in the third quarter, to $24.5 million.

But apparently Fruit of the Loom's logo **never** had a cornucopia.

Twitter user Nick Hinton wrote a long article about it.[27]

Twitter Is Debating Which Fruit Of The Loom Logo Is Right, After Man Points Out You're Probably Remembering It Wrong

If you're not familiar with the Mandela Effect, it's basically when your brain creates false memories, making you think you've seen, heard, or known certain things that are in fact completely untrue. Remember thinking the Berenstain Bears were actually the Berenstein Bears? That's the Mandela Effect. How about spelling *Looney Tunes* as *Looney Toons*? You get the picture. The Mandela Effect is named for the false memory some people share of Nelson Mandela dying in prison in the 1980s, when in reality he died in 2013.

Twitter user @NickHintonn gave us another crazy example of the Mandela Effect last Friday when he pointed out that the Fruit of the Loom logo, which features various fruits in front of a bit of green foliage, definitely doesn't have a cornucopia, despite people very much believing it did.

Nick Hinton
@NickHintonn

The Fruit of the Loom logo has never had a cornucopia in the background!! This is another mind bending Mandela Effect. The 'real' logo just doesn't feel right to me.

FRUIT OF THE LOOM.   FRUIT OF THE LOOM.

7:31 AM · Oct 5, 2019

♡ 23.4K   ♡ 6.9K people are Tweeting about this

Why, again, do so many people (myself included) remember it differently?

And this last one is a real smoking gun to me:

Luke 5:37-38

Luke 5:37-38 in the King James Bible. Many experts remember the verse saying "No man putteth new wine in old wineskins". That's the way so many of us remember the passage. However, now it talks about *bottles* not wineskins. I'm not a Bible scholar but I also remember the passage being about wineskins. This makes sense because that's what they used to hold wine in those days, wineskins. They didn't use bottles back then. In this YouTube clip, the lady making the video claims to have an *original* bible where it clearly says wineskins. It's worth watching.[28]

Here's an image of her Bible…

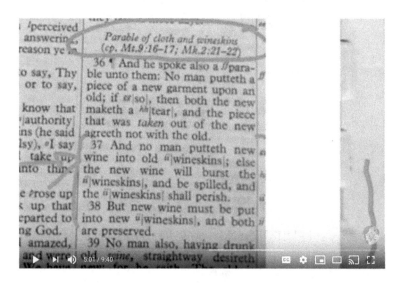

And here's the current version…

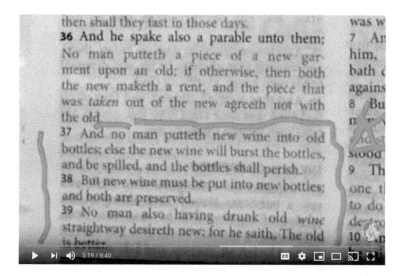

then shall they fast in those days.

36 And he spake also a parable unto them; No man putteth a piece of a new garment upon an old; if otherwise, then both the new maketh a rent, and the piece that was *taken* out of the new agreeth not with the old.

37 And no man putteth new wine into old bottles; else the new wine will burst the bottles, and be spilled, and the bottles shall perish.

38 But new wine must be put into new bottles; and both are preserved.

39 No man also having drunk old wine straightway desireth new: for he saith, The old is better.

This one goes beyond the possibility that we're just 'misremembering' the past. Either someone has changed the King James Bible or there's clearly something else going on here.

To my knowledge *no one* is taking credit for changing the Bible.

These are just some that affect me personally. There are over 400 recorded examples of the Mandela Effect and you can check out more of them here:[29]

I have seen examples of the Mandela Effect where I remember the current version not the Mandela version. Not all of them are accurate to me. But that's just my experience. I would love to know yours.

I have a friend who not only remembers 'one' personal past, but multiple ones. Jobs he did but for which there is no record for and in companies that 'don't exist'. Businesses he's visited and dealt with that have never 'existed'. He also has very vivid dreams of other lives that he feels other 'selves' are living in. Maybe he's just crazy. Maybe he isn't. The thing is, he's one of the most prolific and creative people I've ever met. He's written over 20 books and his intelligence is off the charts, so I can't really discount what he says he's experiencing.

In one of the *Seth* books, author Jane Roberts describes her dying mother 'remembering' a happy marriage with her father. Jane remembers nothing of the sort but speculated that her mother had 'rewritten' her past or had moved into a timeline in which her marriage had been happy.

Denial?

Senility?

Or a genuine shift in universes and timelines?

This is a subject that Jane Roberts discussed at length in all her books, not only the *Seth* ones.

Then again, who knows? Maybe we're just all misremembering everything.

When we look closely at what's really going on 'out there' in the 'outside' world, based on the most cutting-edge quantum physics, we can easily see that it's at least just as possible that we're traveling through the multiverse as it is that we're all misremembering. We know for certain that the particles that make up our bodies are doing it so it just makes sense that we might be too.

As we talked about already, the only 'proof' we *could* have, the only 'evidence' there could be that we are in a different universe is if things are different to the way we remember them to be, such as in the examples above. Some of those examples might speak to you too, or maybe not, as it's really a very personal thing. And, at least for the moment, it's unprovable, since everyone remembers their own, very personal past, and insists it's true.

But, at least for me, I actually see my past changing all the time now, so much so that I don't give it too much thought. There was a period of time, for example, when I lived in a reality where Sylvester Stallone died during the making of *Creed II* (sorry, Sly!). I was really upset about it. I loved all the *Rocky* films and I'm from Philadelphia, so it felt very personal. I also have a lot of respect for Stallone. When it happened, there were all kinds of posts and memes on Facebook and social media. It was going on for quite a while.

Then, all the sudden, it went away. *Creed II* came out; he was still alive and that was the end of it and now I don't give it a second thought. I kind of move around a lot these days. Every morning I focus on raising my energy and vibration and consciously moving to the highest universe possible and, sometimes, there are some pretty big leaps.

I distinctly remember the first time I was aware of the relationship between my vibration and the outside world. It was in 1989. I had just had the most amazing meditation of my life. As soon as I was finished, I turned and noticed the TV out of the corner of my eye. They were showing scenes of the Berlin Wall being demolished. Twenty-eight years of Cold War – war that, in many ways, threatened the survival of the human race more than any other time – came to an end that morning.

I remember feeling instantly that I had just transitioned into a higher vibrational universe from that meditation. I had only been meditating for two years and the thought never occurred to me before that I could change my outer reality by changing the quality of my energy, but at that moment, I was sure that that's what happened.

I find one thing particularly comforting about the notion of quantum immortality. If it is true that CERN or some other events are causing our world to blow up all the time and we just keep migrating from universe to universe when that happens, it's nice to know we keep living!

Think of how amazing that is!

What if every time the world ends, we just keep living our lives as if nothing happened?

Think of what a HUGE burden we can lift off of our shoulders if we don't have to worry about all these idiots killing us! All that fear goes away. We don't have to give up all our power in the form of fear and worry to outside forces. It's so empowering to feel that we're safe from the lunacy of the world! It gives us back an infinite amount of power and control.

Is it true? Who knows? I believe it is and this is how I live my life. Rather than worrying about what's going on 'out there'. I focus on raising my energy and my vibration to the highest level possible, and doing things, which we'll take about in a minute, to consciously bring my energy to the highest universe possible.

That's where all my safety lies, for me personally – in consciously traveling to the highest universe possible and that's what I'd like to invite you to do with me.

7

AN OCEAN OF UNIVERSES

Now that we've come to a point where perhaps you doubt the existence of everything outside your own mind – and perhaps in it as well – and entertain the idea that everything is an illusion, or even non-existent, we can begin to play with some ideas that are even weirder.

Let's say hypothetically for a moment that it's true – that we're moving through different universes all the time. What causes us to move from one universe to another and is it something we can control consciously? Can we use this to our advantage, to create the healthiest, happiest, best life for ourselves in the best world possible?

This is where I want to play a little bit.

I have no solid proof for what I'm about to say, because some things are unprovable. But I do know from my own experiences and from the insights that I've gotten that this is very much how things work for me.

So I say, let's approach these ideas together, as fellow explorers, knowing that anything is possible and also knowing that if we figure something out that can benefit us, it's going to be a HUGE win.

Why? Because the solution to EVERY problem you have and the solution to ALL OF THE WORLD'S PROBLEMS may very well lie in our ability to be conscious universe hoppers. If there's a problem in your life or 'out there' in the 'real' world, simply move to a universe where those problems don't exist.

Maybe it won't be perfect every time or maybe it will, who knows? But there's certainly no harm in giving it a try....

An Ocean of Universes

Imagine your life as a timeline from past to future. Everything that ever happened to you, or will happen, is on this timeline. This is your life in one particular universe. Past is on the left, the present is somewhere in the middle and the future is moving out to the right. Just one long timeline...

Now imagine the timeline for 10 to the power of 500 universes all stacked on top of each other. And let's imagine this represents all the different universes you could be living in or experiencing. Some are great, amazing lives, where you're healthy, happy, prosperous, in love, there's world peace, no pollution, no crime, etc.... You get the picture – utopia!

Then there are other universes where it's a dystopian nightmare. The machines have taken over, wiped out most of the population, blocked the sun from coming in, every second is a struggle for existence – basically hell!

And now imagine all the universes are stacked up on top of each other from worst to best. So the hellish ones are at the very bottom and at the top it's pure heaven. They are stacked on top of each other like a huge, multi-levelled ocean of universes.

• • •

So the question is, which universe are you going to be living in?

Are you going to be in one of the lower, hellish ones or one or the higher, beautiful worlds? What determines your place in the multiverse?

For example, let's take a guy who was running for president. In one version of reality he's trying, but then he gets tired and starts to act in a self-destructive way, or maybe there's some bad publicity about him and he didn't win. In another version, another universe, those negative things didn't happen and he won.

Two totally different versions of the universe for him. Right? Think of how different those universes are and how different his life is going to be from one universe to the other.

Both are universes that exist because *all* universes exist. Our presidential candidate could exist in either of the above universes – and more and they're all completely different, like night and day different, like winter and summer.

So both of these universes are totally different for him, but what about us?

Let's say in the universe where he was president, he did an amazing job and there was peace on earth and everything was beautiful. But in the other version, where he didn't become president and somebody else did, there was war and chaos. It was horrible. Two totally different universes, not just for him but for us!

So the question is, which universe are _we_ going to be in?

Because we can experience both universes. Are we going to be in the war one or the peace one and why?

There are lots of answers to this question and some of them are somewhat philosophical. For example, we may want to be in the 'war version', to learn something very important about ourselves or about life. In the war version we may discover how brave we are or how heroic or how strong we are. Or we may develop certain skills and strengths in the war version that we otherwise wouldn't have learned.

So maybe our soul, or the higher versions of ourselves, might want to be in a less desirable situation because it benefits us on a soul level in some way. Or we may want to be in the war version because our soul or higher self has a strong desire to help people that are suffering and our soul may choose to be in the war-torn world to give us an opportunity to help others.

Or we may have developed a belief early in life that "life is hell" or "war is inevitable". This belief took root early in childhood, based on something we heard our parents or teachers say. We then developed an unconscious belief that life would be hard, we would struggle and there would be war when we got older because "war is inevitable". In this scenario we might be 'willing' ourselves on an unconscious level to the lower existence.

So there are lots of issues at play and we can't always make the assumption that a seemingly negative situation is ALL bad. We might be learning something from it that will help us grow as people and on a soul level. We might agree on a soul level to have negative experiences for some positive reason. Some people say that we know the events in our childhood, before we are born. This makes sense, since the soul exists outside of time and space, it's conceivable that we might 'know' all of our life experiences before they happen and our 'job' is to experience them to 'embody the knowing'.

Both Louise Hay and Oprah were sexually abused as children. This is one of the worst tragedies a child could experience. Is it possible that they had knowledge on a soul level that this was going to happen to them before they were born? It's unthinkable.

But...

Both Louise Hay and Oprah went on to heal themselves from these tragedies and then dedicated their lives to helping and healing as many people as they could. One could argue that they've helped millions of people around the world heal. Would they have still been so motivated and dedicated to helping to heal the world if they had not suffered the traumas they did? Who can say? They would certainly be different people if they hadn't experienced the abuse, but who can say if that's a good thing or not?

I suffered trauma and abuse in my early childhood, and I know it has motivated me throughout my life to evolve and grow and also to help others. At times it has given me boundless energy and strength to persevere.

But let's put all that aside for a second and just look at the events of life in a black-and-white, good-and-bad kind of way. Aside from some of these less obvious reasons why we might choose to live in a world where we experience pain, suffering or failure, what are some of the other influences that might affect which universe we are going to be experiencing?

In my experience, the biggest influence that will determine which universe we exist in is our vibration.

Let's go back to this analogy of an ocean of universes stacked on top of each other. So the worst, most hellish universe is at the bottom and the best, most heavenly universes are at the top.

From my experience, this ocean of universes functions very similar to an ocean of water. In a typical ocean of water, the lower you go, the harder it is. The lower you go, the darker it is and the pressure gets worse and worse, to the point that it's bone crushing. If we were at the bottom of a deep ocean, we would be crushed in minutes.

Then the higher up you go in the ocean, the easier it is. The pressure gets less and less, we can see better and better and at the very top, we can breathe!

Now what determines how higher or low we will be in an ocean of water? Our density, which is another way of saying our vibration. If you look at a rock, it's a solid, the molecules in the rock are vibrating slowly, it's dense and it will sink – all the way to the bottom of the water.

No let's look at a balloon with air. Air is less dense than water. Air has a higher vibration than water, so a balloon floats to the top. Now let's look at a scuba diver. A scuba diver is going to have both a belt of weights and a balloon that he can inflate or deflate at will. The balloon is called a buoyancy compensator. Where is the scuba diver going to be in the ocean?

If the diver wants to move higher, he will inflate his balloon a bit, and that raises his vibration and he moves up. If he wants to dive deeper, he will deflate the balloon, and he then becomes more dense. With his vibration lower and denser, he sinks.

Now let's look at our 'ocean of universes'. In the same way, the lower we go, the harder and more hellish the universe is. We could argue that, in a sense, it's a denser universe and if we are very dense, that is, our vibration is very low, we would sink down to the lower universes. The opposite is also true. If our vibration is very high, if we are less dense, we will drift higher and higher to better, more high vibrational universes.

So how do we do that? How do we raise our vibration in the ocean of universes?

It's all in our ability to channel energy...

LET'S GET HOPPING

8

CHANNELING SUCCESS

FOR THOUSANDS OF YEARS, eastern medical traditions have been studying our subtle life-force energy, also known as chi, ki, qi or prana.

Many medical professionals scoff at the idea of chi because they don't believe that it's there. But radio waves have been there since the beginning of time, but we didn't even know we had radio waves until a few hundred years ago. In fact, there are lots of 'invisible' forms of energy that we're discovering all the time. As science develops instruments to detect these subtle waves, they are 'discovered'.

We have a subtle life-force energy current that runs through our bodies that we can't detect with our 'normal' senses, but it is there, nonetheless. Eastern medicine has been studying this subtle life-force energy for thousands of years, and, according to experts in the field, our chi is at the essence of the mind–body connection.

Ever wonder how thought creates movement? To me, this is one of the greatest miracles in the world and something that has always puzzled me. How does a thought—an invisible, nonphysical notion—translate to movement in our bodies?

We think, "I want to pick up that apple", and that invisible thought somehow creates movement. Neurons fire and nerves stimulate muscle contractions in an amazingly complex and coordinated sequence and the apple gets picked up.

Truly miraculous!

Chinese medicine has its own explanation. Our thoughts are a *force*. Not a strong enough force to 'move matter' – at least not for most of us – but a force strong enough to move chi energy. Chi energy then creates an energetic ripple that affects the electrons in our brain cells. That causes our brain cells to "fire," sending messages to other brain cells, which results in nerves firing and muscles contracting. So, our life-force energy, a subtle form of energy that responds to our desires, is the interface between thought and movement.

This subtle life-force energy circulates through the body along discrete, invisible pathways, just like blood travels through arteries and veins.

Energy channels in the body...

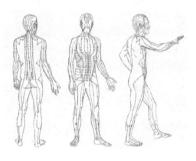

Known in acupuncture as 'meridians', or 'nadis', these pathways keep the body working smoothly. In traditional forms of medicine, disease originates when blockages occur in these energy channels.

Treating disease requires *removing* the energy blockage and restoring the flow. That's what acupuncturists are doing with needles: they're unblocking your energy channels.

You're at your healthiest and most vibrant when your energy channels are open and flowing freely.

When you have blockages, your entire body will suffer as a result. You'll feel exhausted, you'll be stressed, and you'll get sick.

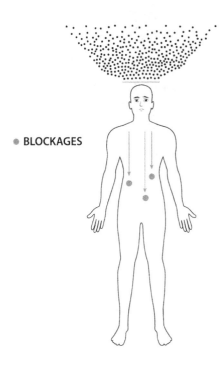

BLOCKAGES

Blockages in energy channels. Higher energies not able to pass through the body. Vibration lowering, getting denser. Vitality, health, happiness decreasing.

Getting your life-force pathways open and flowing is the best way to create health, stay fit, and boost your vitality. Because when your energy channels are open and flowing it allows this precious life-force energy to flow to all the areas in your body that need it.

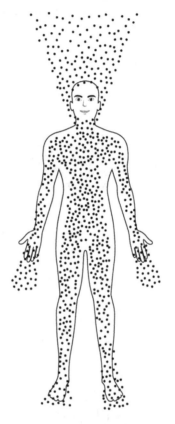

Energy channels open. Higher energies able to enter and pass through the body. Vibration raising. Health, happiness and vitality increasing.

After I did that 21-day water fast that I mentioned in the beginning of the book, my energy channels were open and flowing. I didn't know it at the time, but apparently fasting is one of the best ways to clean out and open up your energy channels.

Jesus fasted for 40 days in the desert and Buddha fasted and meditated for six months under a tree. I have a close friend who is a qigong master. His name is Robert Peng. When he was 17 his teacher put him in an underground room in a monastery in China where he stayed and fasted and meditated for 100 days. After that experience, he developed the ability to transmit energy and he now uses this ability to heal people of diseases that are typically incurable. I've experienced his energy and so has my daughter and my wife. When he touches you, it feels like an electric current is passing through your body. Your entire body starts shaking. It's unreal.

And it's not just chi or life-force energy that runs through these channels, it's also the higher energy aspects of yourself.

What I've learned is that there are unbelievably high vibrational energies that can enter your body, but they will only do so when your energy channels are open enough to channel the energy through your body. If the channels are blocked or not open enough to handle the full transmission, these energies will not come in at all.

It's possible that both Jesus and Buddha were gods or divine incarnations, originating in realities outside of our 'normal' ones and manifesting in the material plane. Obviously, the Christian viewpoint is that Jesus was God in human form and some Buddhists think the same of Buddha. It's certainly possible. I would add though that what enabled their physical bodies to fully manifest their 'Godself' in this world was the exercises they did, such as fasting and meditating, to open their channels enough to allow that energy to come into their bodies, without harming their physical bodies.

Think of lightning. It's a super powerful, high vibrational energy. We've all heard stories of people being struck by lightning and living. But usually lightning just fries people to smithereens.

Why is that? Why do some people live? Because they were able to somehow channel the energy through their bodies and into the ground. Maybe it bounced off their zipper (ouch!) then the steel tip of their shoes and then into the ground. Or, in some other way, the lightning was able to make it all the way through their bodies and so they lived. But if the energy can't make it through a blockage in your body, it hits the block like a tsunami hitting up against a dam, the dam bursts and you die.

It's the same with the higher non-physical energies. Those energies include this chi, or life-force energy we're talking about, but it also includes the higher energies of our soul, higher self and other higher energies.

Buddha, Jesus, people like Robert Peng and possibly many others can channel these energies. But they've all done work on their bodies to handle the transmission. If those higher energies come into your body and you can't handle them, it can be life-threatening.

As I talked about in the beginning of this book, I experienced firsthand how opening your energy channels can allow higher vibrational energies into the body. I felt like a God force was living in my body for a few days. But it didn't last. And that's because I couldn't keep channeling the energy. My energy channels didn't stay open enough to keep that higher vibrational energy running through me.

I discovered years later that there was a reason for this. After the 21-day water fast, my body was highly purified and my energy channels were open enough to handle higher energies running through them. But what I discovered the hard way is that when you have no food for 21 days, your digestion completely shuts down and your peristalsis stops. Peristalsis is the gentle rhythmic motion of your intestines that allows for food to pass through you. Because it shuts down you have to take steps to make sure you have a bowel movement within the first two days after you start eating again.

I didn't know that, I didn't do that and that's not what happened. What's more, for about five days all I ate were persimmons, because I had completely lost interest in food. But I did eat the persimmons because there happened to be a big box of them on the table and every once in a while when I passed by I ate one. Then I reached that superhuman state I described and I didn't think about going to the bathroom at all. I discovered years later that persimmons cause constipation!

Anyway, I hadn't gone to the bathroom for about 10 days and I developed a block in my intestines. The block didn't allow me to handle the transmission of the higher energies that were running through my body. Because I couldn't channel the energy, my nerves started shaking and it affected my body, mind and nervous system in various ways. As soon as it became dangerous for me to have that energy running through me it left. It didn't leave to 'punish me' or because it 'no longer loved me'. It simply left because I couldn't handle the transmission anymore. If your channels are not open, your 'higher self' will simply not allow the higher energies to come into your body in the first place – AND THAT'S FOR YOUR PROTECTION.

The Benefits of Staying Unblocked

Since my 'awakening' in 2006 I've been known to spend hours a day opening up my energy channels through meditations, visualizations, prayers, emotional healing and other practices.

I find that every second I spend in unblocking is worth it. I see tremendous differences between my 'blocked' and 'unblocked' states on a daily basis. That is, between how open my energy channels are and how my life is flowing. When my energy is flowing nicely through my energy channels, my life is flowing and when it's blocked, some aspect of my life is blocked too, and I can tell that I've sunk a little in the ocean of universes and that I've moved into a lower energy existence.

When that happens, I don't fight what's 'going on in the world' that's causing me problems, because that's just 'the story', that's just 'the ocean'. The problem is with the diver – me. So, I become just like a scuba diver that needs to adjust his buoyancy compensator.

I go back to raising my energy, I step up, I rise up and then the problem seems to go away either on its own or it gets resolved easily. The daily relationship of cause and effect between how open I am and how much my life is flowing is so direct, the feedback is so immediate and uncanny that I don't even give it a second thought anymore. Problems that might seem insurmountable when you're floating at one level will completely disappear in a single day, often in a single instant, at a higher level, and I no longer give it a second thought.

Aside from other more philosophical considerations about why we would want to have problems or choose to be in a low vibrational universe, raising your vibration is the greatest way to transition into the highest universes possible. And you raise your vibration when you open your energy channels.

The more open your energy channels, the higher your vibration will be and the higher you will float in the 'ocean of universes'.

It's like the difference between a bowling ball and sponge in an ocean. The ball will sink because the water can't flow through. It's solid and dense. But a sponge has lots of holes for where the water can flow through. When we open our channels, we become like a sponge and the ocean of higher energies can flow through us and we drift higher and higher.

Unblocking your energy channels and keeping them open and flowing is the single greatest thing you can do, to live an amazing life in an amazing world.

Our energy channels become blocked through fear, negativity, stress and toxins. The pathways constrict, inhibiting the flow of higher energies through our bodies and increasing our density.

Staying blocked is like attaching a ball and chain to your foot.

Staying blocked is like having mafia-style concrete boots, or like tying an anchor to yourself. You can't rise higher when you're weighed down.

The sad irony is that when we want to change something about ourselves or the world and we do it through fighting in a way that causes us to feel angry, hostile, stressed, powerless, resentful, doomed, overwhelmed or thwarted, we actually make the problem worse. Because all those negative feelings are blocking our energy channels, lowering our vibration and causing us to sink down to lower vibrational universes, where the problems are even worse.

The solution to EVERY problem is to unblock your energy channels and raise your vibration. Because the answer to EVERY problem already exists in a higher vibrational universe and it's up to you to get there.

We need to unblock our energy channels and we can do that with things like:

Fasting
Eating 'clean'
Meditation
Visualization

Breath work
Grounding
Conscious love making/redirecting our sexual energy
Charity/selfless service
Art, creativity, inspiration
Emotional healing
Positive emotional states
Reprogramming limiting beliefs and mind–body practices, like

- Yoga
- Tai chi
- Qigong

This is just a short list and we will talk about some of these techniques in detail in the coming pages.

It's worth noting that energy researcher Dawson Church, Ph.D., author of *The Genie in Your Genes*, has found some tangible evidence of the existence of our energy channels.

He says:

> Studies show that points on the life-force meridians have much lower electrical resistance (averaging 10,000 ohms at the center of the point) when compared to the surrounding skin (which averages a much higher 3,000,000 ohms). Among other characteristics, acupuncture points propagate acoustic sound better than does the surrounding skin. They also emit small amounts of light and greater amounts of carbon dioxide. When the points are stimulated with a low-frequency current, the body responds by producing endorphins and cortisol. When they are stimulated with a higher-frequency current, the body produces serotonin and norepinephrine. When the surrounding skin receives the same current, these neurochemicals are not produced.

So, it's clear that cutting-edge medical science, from open-minded, creative researchers, is recognizing the validity of the

5,000-year-old study of chi energy and our subtle life-force energy channels.

What's common to nearly all mind–body practices is that they use visualization and/or breathing techniques to direct life-force energy to different parts of the body and unblock energy channels. Remember that life-force energy is moved and controlled *by your mind*.

In yoga, tai chi and qigong you're using breathing, visualization, and gentle movement or stretching to direct life force through the body. In guided meditations, you're using breathing and/or visualization to circulate your life-force energy. As you direct life-force energy to various parts of your body, it clears out blockages, so that your channels are open and flowing.

When our channels are open and flowing, we're then channeling higher vibrational energies into and through our bodies. These higher energies, which include many of the higher aspects of ourselves, will cause our vibration to rise and allow us to flow, easily and effortlessly, into the highest, most beautiful universes available to us.

9

LIFE BEYOND YOUR SENSES

MEDITATION COMBINED with specific visualizations (which we'll talk about in a minute) are the best ways I know to open your energy channels and to raise your vibration.

But I just want to talk about meditation first, because meditation is SO MUCH MORE than just a mere relaxation technique.

Meditation is the single most important and meaningful thing you can do in your life. Why? Because it is the ONLY time you are awake and aware and alive and NOT USING YOUR FIVE MATERIAL SENSES!

The single thing I am most grateful for in my life is that I became addicted to meditation back in 1987 and I've been meditating pretty much every day since. The more time you spend outside of your senses the more things just start to make 'sense'.

As we know, our physical senses are lying to us.

Meditation is the only time we go beyond our senses. It is the only time we are able to experience any semblance of a 'true' reality and see the omniverse as the ocean of potentiality that it really is.

As we've talked about already, when we see a tree, it's just vibrations. When we see a person, it's just vibrations.

In reality, these vibrations are not even moving, because time is not going from past to future; we're just seeing it that way. It's like a movie. A movie is made of thousands of still images. None of the images are moving; it's just the projector that's running the images across the screen, creating the illusion of movement.

If the projector runs the images forward, then it looks like the images are moving forward. If the projector runs the images backward, it looks like the images are moving backward. But what's actually happening is that the individual images are not moving at all. When we watch a movie there is the illusion of movement, that we watched some of the events 'already' and the rest of the events 'have not happened yet'.

But what's going on is that the entire movie, from past to future, has already been created and it's just the projector that's moving the still images.

A digital movie on your computer isn't even images.

It's just a bunch of zeros and ones that tell a computer to fire a bunch of colored pixels on your screen to light up in the correct coordinated sequence to create the illusion of images moving in front of you.

It's just a bunch of zeros and ones that tell a computer to fire a bunch of vibrations onto your speakers in the correct coordinated sequence to create the illusion of voices, music and sound effects.

The 'world' is very much like that – wave up, wave down in a multidimensional 'quantum foam' that fires a bunch of vibrations into your consciousness to create the illusion of light, sound, smell, taste, warmth, movement, pleasure, pain and even 'memory'.

And in fact, if you look at dreams, you can see that they are similar to 'reality'. You see and hear things as if they are 'really real'. You believe the things that are happening as if they're real. You might be dreaming that you're at a school that you've never been to before, but for some strange reason, you all of a sudden believe that you've been going to that school for years. The people in the dream might be people that you've never seen or heard of before, but you already believe they are your best friends, or worst enemies, depending on the dream.

Whatever the drama is that's going on in the dream feels real and you might be totally engaged in it. That's because the same mechanisms your brain and mind use to create the false reality of this 'real' life are creating the dreams as well. It might also feel like the dream is going on for hours when in fact the whole dream may have only been a few seconds, like the example I gave earlier of the guillotine dream. That's because time doesn't exist in a dream, it's just an illusion, in the same way time doesn't exist in the 'outside' world and is just an illusion as well. And the illusion works, up to a point.

The movie *The Truman Show* made this point beautifully. Truman ('true man') completely accepted the reality that he was in. Why wouldn't he? We accept *ours*. Until, that is, the cracks in reality begin to appear, like they do for so many people, like they did for me in 2006. Only when the cracks were too big for Truman not to notice did he seek to escape. Until reality turned into 'reality' he didn't even realize that there was anything to escape from.

And up until the cracks began to be impossible to ignore, and showed him that there was something else 'beyond', there wasn't any other reality to escape *to*.

It's all just a bunch of waves of energy – signals to your senses.

There's no actual 'things' out there and nothing is 'happening' except, for want of a better term, 'in your head'. It's only your mind that interprets the signals as images and then plays them sequentially for you from past to future.

The events you see with your senses are *not* happening in front of your eyes. Past wasn't in the past and future events are not in the future. The present is happening *now*. The future is happening *now*. The past is happening *now*. It's just our minds that experience the images/events in a sequential fashion from past to future, but that's just an illusion.

It's like that scene in the movie *The Matrix* when a spoon is being bent without being touched and the little boy says, "There is no spoon, it's just your mind that's bending."

In truth, *THERE IS NO SPOON*, or anything else for that matter; it's just your mind, creating this illusion.

The rishis of India who created the Upanishads got their information from what we in the West would call 'revelation' and that came from meditating hours a day. Their message is clear and consistent. The world is an illusion; it's just made of "God stuff", as am I, as are you.

But the only way to get any semblance of any real information is to take all this a step further and that happens when you are experiencing life *outside of your mind and senses*. Because beyond the 'realm of illusion' there is a 'higher realm'. Something exists and it's very real and it's amazing. Normal physical, material sense experiences pale in comparison. But the only way to experience it is outside of your material senses.

You have to transcend your mind and senses. You have to go peek outside of the bubble of 'reality' you're in. And once you do, you're hooked.

The crossover comes when you experience awareness outside of your material senses – 'beyond the bubble'. Because every sensation that we experience is not coming from the 'outside world', it's coming from something beyond our 'normal' perception.

Think of sex. We've used this analogy before. I like using sex as an example, because we all think it feels great. But as we talked about before, if you were numb from the waist down, it wouldn't feel good at all. Sex wouldn't feel like anything. So sex doesn't feel good in and of itself. The sex 'act' is meaningless outside the 'signals' that create the illusion. If we were able to go into that part of your brain that's in charge of sex and stimulate the brain cells that would be stimulated if you were having sex, it would feel just as amazing as the 'real' thing. But let's be clear, it's not sex in this case that would be making you feel good. It's just the excitation of those neurons.

Here is something to understand…

That feeling of sex, that amazing feeling of pleasure and enjoyment, already exists, somewhere inside you ALL THE TIME.

Stimulating the neurons in charge of the sexual feeling doesn't cause you to feel great. It just somehow allows you to access the feelings of pleasure THAT ARE ALREADY INSIDE YOU.

It's almost as if the neurons in charge of sex are like a lock and stimulating those neurons acts as a key that unlocks it and gives you temporary access to the amazing feelings that are already inside you. It's like our brain is the gatekeeper to these feelings, shutting them off to our normal awareness and then allowing you to experience them under certain circumstances.

But when you're willing to experience life beyond your material senses, and you take the appropriate action, you bypass the part of your brain that is the gatekeeper and you access the feelings that are already inside you, without having to stimulate those neurons or unlock that part of the brain. And that's true for all pleasurable feelings.

The feeling of a great massage, an amazing meal, skiing down the most perfect slope, or surfing the greatest wave, winning the lottery and the further feelings of power and freedom all those experiences might give us.

In fact, in the Upanishads it's said that orgasm is the feeling that God has all the time while in the throes of infinite and eternal creation of all realities.

That's not such a bad place to be.

ANY pleasurable feeling or experience that you can imagine is already 'inside' you somewhere, because EVERY experience already exists. It's already a part of your nature and bypassing your material senses is the way to access them.

Bypassing Material Senses to the Realm of Bliss

Material sensual experiences pale in comparison to what you can experience beyond your senses by DIRECTLY accessing your bliss. In fact, I never really understood what the word bliss meant until I experienced it one day in meditation. There's no way to express in words that feeling and how amazing it is. And suffice it to say that after that day, I no longer cared for material sense experiences the same way. I know that anything I experience in the 'outside' world, with my body and senses, will pale in comparison to what I am able to experience when I bypass them in meditation.

That's why I say that nothing is more important than meditation. To me, there's meditation and then there's everything else that's not meditation, which I view as a watered-down version of enjoyment.

That feeling of bliss makes you start to feel connected – connected to something beyond 'this' world. You start to feel more at home outside of your mind and senses. And you start to get a sense of what life is like after 'death'. Many people have a sense of these possibilities already, a sense so great that they feel 'trapped' by the material body and its material senses.

AND the body needs food, clothing, shelter, sleep, the right temperature, blah, blah, blah.

AND all this requires money and if we don't have the money to satisfy the body's needs or find some other way to satisfy its needs, we suffer.

AND if we don't have the resources to satisfy our body's needs, we become beggars or flatterers to the people we think can help us, and in various ways compromise our purity and integrity to get the things we need.

AND there's no end to the body's needs. And if the body is unhealthy it's yet another ball-and-chain that you have to drag with you wherever you go. If a boulder lands on someone's foot and crushes it, they would be cast into a world of pain, to which there is no escape, unless they take some kind of drug to numb the pain.

And this is exactly what most of us do, take some kind of drug to numb the pain, whether the pain is physical, mental or emotional, we all, for the most part, drug ourselves through life. If we don't drug ourselves with chemistry and pharmaceuticals, or alcohol and drugs, we drug ourselves with food, or sex, or TV, social media and we turn all these things into addictions. Even the endless pursuit of knowledge can be an addiction.

But when you're in a deep state of meditation, you no longer feel trapped 'inside' your body or trapped in the illusory world of your mind and material senses. You begin to feel like this place of bliss is exactly where you go when you die. Because to me the only difference between life and death is that in life you're trapped in a pretend world, a make-believe world, a dream you usually can't get out of. When you're in a deep meditation you are out of that world, you are free and I'm pretty sure that's exactly what death feels like. Jesus said, "I die daily". And I'm pretty sure this is what he meant by that. It just makes sense. He left the fake, dream world of the mind and senses and went to what's real. Sometimes I'm in an infinite place of bliss and peace, where there's no time, no fear and no worries.

I believe this is available to all of us, it's our birthright and all we have to do is claim it.

Death has completely lost its sting for me. If I were to die, I couldn't be happier. I would only be sad that I wouldn't be as accessible to my kids and for any pain that my leaving might cause my family and friends. But, other than that, for me personally, I would love it. That being said, I don't mind life either. In fact, it keeps getting better. I have an awesome life and I wouldn't trade places with anyone. *But I have no attachment to it whatsoever.* I recognize that it's not real, it's just a dream. I'm happy to play the game, but when it's time to go, I'm there!

I don't have a bucket list, there's nowhere that I need to be and nothing I need to do. Anything I do and anywhere I go is with my body and my material senses and these experiences pale in comparison to bliss and joy outside of the material senses. Material sense pleasures are like having fun with a bag over your head. It's dull and suffocating and somewhat lifeless compared to the pleasure you can experience when you're free from the confines of your body, the material senses and the illusory world.

Because the reality is that no matter how good our lives are, we are in a kind of prison. If you can't escape your mind and material senses and the fake world it's creating for you, you're in a prison. The definition of prison isn't how good or bad the prison is. Prisons can have iron bars, or gold bars. The definition of a prison is that you can't leave of your own free will. You're being *forced* to stay. The prison could be good or bad, but if you can't leave, you're in prison.

Your prison might be like a real jail cell or it might be like living at the nicest beach resort in Hawaii, but either way *if you can't escape, it's a prison*. And we all have several different strategies for trying to escape, if at least temporarily. But these methods all extract a heavy price, through toxifying our bodies, creating addictions, exhausting us or dissipating our vital life-force energy – all blocking our energy channels, lowering our energy and causing us to sink to lower, less enjoyable universes.

By way of contrast, meditation teaches you how to escape in a way that only strengthens you, because when you leave, you're going to your REAL home, not just another delusional reality. It's calming, soothing, energizing and revitalizing and it's giving you what you truly long for in your heart and soul. When you learn how to leave the world of the mind and material senses at will, through meditation, you're no longer in jail.

Only meditation can teach you how to leave, because meditation is the ONLY time you're awake and aware and alive and NOT in your mind and material senses.

And you get better and better at it over time. And your meditations become deeper and more satisfying over time. You also start to develop a 'sixth', non-material sense, a deep sense of *intuition* and nothing can make you feel safer and more relaxed and help you be more successful in life than a highly developed sense of intuition.

10

GETTING THE GUIDANCE YOU NEED

ON ONE OF my favorite bike rides, there is a short but steep hill on a dirt road in farm country just past some local wineries. Although the hill only takes about two or three minutes to climb, it's so intense that I feel a tremendous sense of accomplishment when I reach the top.

I usually celebrate by raising my hands in the air and letting myself fly down the other side of the hill without my hands on the handlebars. Maybe that's not the best idea, but it's fun. I feel so alive when I'm sailing down that hill.

One day, after reaching the top, I was about to do my celebratory coast down the other side, when a little voice inside my head said, "No. Don't do that. Keep your hands on the bars." I listened, and right after this intuition struck me, a six-foot-tall kangaroo came out of the woods and charged right at me.

He wasn't trying to attack me. Kangaroos are like 200-pound squirrels: when they're startled, they'll just charge across the road. While hitting a squirrel can make you feel bad, smashing into a kangaroo is a whole other story. He was just trying to get to the other side of the road, and he wasn't too bothered by the fact that he might have to trample me in the process.

I was already moving at full speed when he charged. I had less than a second to respond. I swerved quickly and started heading for the far side of the road. Thankfully, there were no cars.

I also slammed on my brakes and felt the back of my bike lifting as I went into a skid. I managed to turn the bike almost completely around and I landed in a ditch with nothing but some scrapes from sliding on the road.

I hesitate to imagine what would have happened if I had had my hands in the air, like I usually do. There's no way I could have controlled my bike, and I would have crashed headfirst into that kangaroo. While kangaroos are normally peaceful animals, they do have sharp talons on their hind legs and routinely disembowel dogs or other predators when they feel threatened.

So, what *was* that little voice inside my head that saved my life?

And what made me listen to it?

The Voice Within

Maybe you've had a life-saving experience like mine. We've all heard of remarkable stories where 'gut feelings' saved people's lives and where that experience changed them forever. These 'gut feelings' are a manifestation of our intuition, our 'sixth sense', and although it's not been widely studied, it's an amazing faculty, an asset that we are all born with and something we can develop and cultivate.

If you're not sure whether intuition is for real, consider this quote:

> *"Research in human pattern recognition and decision making suggests that there is a 'sixth sense' through which humans can detect and act*

on unique patterns without consciously and intentionally analyzing them."

Where's the quote from?

The Office of Naval Research for the United States Department of Defense.

That's right; the U.S. Navy's research department is so interested in developing this sixth sense that in 2019 it began a $3.85 million, four-year research project into the understanding of intuition.[1]

The reason the Navy is interested in intuition is because of the overwhelming number of soldiers and sailors who've made life-saving decisions based on a hunch. In one case, a staff sergeant saved the lives of 17 civilians in a café because he sensed something odd about a would-be bomber. An entire Canadian company of soldiers survived an ambush in Afghanistan based on their intuition that they were wandering into a possible trap. Belief in intuition permeates the business world, as well.

A poll from *PRWeek* and Burson-Marsteller suggests that most CEOs rely on their intuition when making important decisions.[2]

But polls and anecdotal stories aren't the only reason the U.S. Navy wants to learn more about the sixth sense.

The stress research institute HeartMath in California has looked carefully into the phenomenon of intuition. In one study, they had subjects sit in front of a blank computer screen. Occasionally, the computer would flash an image. Some were pleasant scenes, of nature, for example, while others were upsetting, such as a photo of an autopsy.

As the images flashed by, the HeartMath researchers carefully monitored the volunteers' brains and hearts to see when and how they might respond to the images.

An initial surprising finding was that the heart responded before the brain did. The first reaction came not from the mind as you might expect, but from the heart.

But far more remarkable was the fact that both the heart and the brain responded BEFORE THE DISTURBING IMAGE EVEN APPEARED![3]The computer was set to produce the images in totally random and unpredictable order, yet the volunteers 'knew' whether the image would be pleasant or upsetting milliseconds before it appeared on the screen. Based on the results, the researchers concluded that "the body's perceptual apparatus is continuously scanning the future".

Your intuition is very real indeed, as you've probably suspected from incidents in your own life. It's something we are all born with but that many of us lose over time. Intuition atrophies, like a muscle that's never used. Our society simply doesn't encourage the development and use of intuition, so people don't actively exercise it, so it just gets weaker.

What's different about this sixth sense from the material senses is that it's a *nonphysical* sense, and therefore not bound by time and space. With our material senses, we can only perceive what's directly around us or touching us; we can only see, hear, smell, taste, and touch what's within range of our physical perception, and what is physically happening 'in the moment'.

In contrast our sixth sense lets us perceive things that will happen, have happened, or are happening somewhere else in 'the world', or more accurately, in 'the worlds'.

Our intuition is a *quantum sense* – so it can accurately assess the future, simply because the future is, in actuality, happening as we speak.

Intuition and Survival

The material senses exist for several good reasons:

1. They give us access to information
2. They give us a 'picture' with which to paint reality
3. They help ensure our physical survival

The material senses are connected to the 'rational' mind to help us, literally, 'make sense' of it all. If our material senses give us accurate information about potential material threats, they can help us stay and feel safe.

It's the same with your quantum senses. They too can 'perceive ahead', but at another level. They're connected to, for want of a better term, our 'non-rational mind', but it's all in the service of our physical survival.

So, it's in our best interests to add the data from the quantum sense of intuition, even if it's just for the sake of having one more channel of information. Cultivating the latent potential of your intuition is one of the best ways to help you feel safe in your day-to-day life.

Imagine having a developed, reliable and 'far-seeing' intuition that always 'knew' what was going to happen to you not only in the next few moments but in the days or years 'ahead'?

You could be walking home from work and your intuition might tell you to turn left instead of right. 'You', or rather your 'rational mind', might think, "That's ridiculous. I always walk home turning right here; it's a shorter and more direct route" – which is a perfectly reasonable conclusion given the information available from your material senses and the 'memory' of your prior experiences.

But what you may not know – what you have no way of knowing 'rationally' – is that if you turn right, you'll be caught in the crossfire of a madman with a gun. Your quantum intuition can scan the nearby 'futures' and pick this up, but if you're not able to 'hear' the message or you don't 'listen', you can't benefit from the information. Intuitive information is just as valid, perhaps even more valid that material sensory information, but it's non-rational. If you have no knowledge of, or *respect* for, your non-rational mind, your rational mind will reject the information even if that means you end up shot.

Melinda Jacobs, my good friend, *Gabriel Method* coach and intuitive healer, experienced firsthand just how powerful listening to intuition can be.

She was in a movie theater in Aurora, Colorado in 2012 about to watch a midnight screening of *The Dark Knight Rises* when all of a sudden she felt an extreme uneasiness in her stomach.

She knew something wasn't right. She could feel it intuitively, and she left the theater at once. That was on the ill-fated night of the Aurora, Colorado shootings. After she left, a gunman launched tear gas into the theater and then proceeded to gun down members of the audience. Twelve people were killed and 70 wounded. Her highly developed intuition kept her out of harm's way.

Melinda was fortunate because even though intuition is a non-material sense, it still communicates through the material body, in her case, through a powerful and literal *gut feeling*. What's more, Melinda respected what that sense was telling her. Her rational mind said, "I don't know how you work, but I've learned to trust you, so we're out of here!"

We place so much emphasis on the material senses and the rational mind, knowledge and intelligence, but in many cases these faculties pale in comparison to intuition, especially when it comes to safety.

But it's not *just* safety.

Intuition as Tool

Intuition can help you achieve your life's goals and purpose. It can help you be successful in relationships, business, investing, health and fitness; pretty much every aspect of your life can be transformed with intuition. Intuition *works*. And intuition doesn't just detect 'bad' futures any more than your olfactory sense detects 'bad' smells. Intuition can lead you away from a garbage dump, but it can also lead you to a garden of earthly and, in some cases, non-earthly delights.

But for many, intuition is a tough sell.

It's very difficult to understand a sense that you don't have.

Imagine you were transported to a world where no one had eyes. You were the only one. People would think you were some kind of psychic or mystic or medium. They might even call you a magician or a sorcerer. Even if you gave accurate, consistent and demonstrably good information, average people would have no understanding as to how you performed your 'magic'.

How could you possibly know how many people are in the room without touching them, hearing them or smelling them? How could you possibly know how many trees are in the yard, without touching them? Nothing could be simpler or easier for *you*. You *see* them. But everyone else on the planet could not possibly understand. You could explain that you see the light bouncing off of them and they might say, what is light?

You'd have to say something like, "It's like warmth, a bit," but that would hardly be adequate. And how would you describe colors, and shading, the difference between 'shiny' and 'matt', hue, saturation and chroma? They'd either make you a prophet, burn you at the stake or lock you up in a laboratory for the rest of your life – or all three. You have to experience a sense in order to understand it but once you do, it makes total 'sense'.

In the same way, when you have well-developed intuition, you just KNOW what to do. Because your 'sixth' sense is working. How did Melinda know to leave that movie theater? Simple, she *knew* in the same way you might have known that the carpet was red. She used one of her senses: her sixth sense.

If your sixth sense is operational, you're not a 'psychic' or a 'medium'. You're not a 'witch' or a 'sorcerer'. You don't have any 'supernatural' powers. You're just using the God-given sense that we all have but that most of us have effectively lost for the most part.

If you have a fully developed intuition, you can relax and let your intuition guide you through the ocean of universes and timelines within the available 'range' of potentialities. Your intuition will tell you who to do business with, what stocks to buy, where to buy real estate, who you can trust and how to stay out of danger. You'll be directed to your business partners, teachers, soulmates and true friends. The list of benefits is endless, and it's all courtesy of your own intuitive guidance. Intuition is truly a gift that keeps on giving. And all these abilities are possible by merely tapping into a sense-perception mechanism that most of us don't even realize we have. You just have to build that intuitive muscle up a bit.

Building the Intuitive Muscle

When a child is born with a lazy eye, the ophthalmologist will recommend an eye patch for the good eye. Why is that?

The 'muscles' in the lazy eye are weak, so, to compensate, as the child relies more on the good eye, its muscles get stronger and stronger and the lazy eye gets weaker and weaker. So the ophthalmologist puts a patch on the stronger eye. The patch forces the child to focus and control the lazy eye, developing the muscles of that eye, so it will step up to the same level as the stronger one. Eventually, both eyes will be able to work together.

Our atrophied sixth sense is much like a lazy 'third eye'. It has gotten so weak that it can't operate at the same level as the stronger material senses, and therefore can't compete with those senses for the attention of the rational mind that we've come to rely on – to overly rely on.

So, the way to strengthen your sixth sense is to put a "patch" on your other five senses. And that's exactly what's happening when you're meditating.

As we said, meditation is the act of being awake and aware, and not using your five senses. It's like you're 'tuned in' at another level. As you sit quietly with your eyes closed, and not using your material senses, you begin to perceive the world and your surroundings through a different avenue. As you stop 'relying' so much on your material senses for the act of perceiving, you begin to rely on, and thus strengthen, your sixth sense.

Numerous studies demonstrate that the brains of meditators get bigger – actually gain mass – in areas related to emotional sensitivity and that meditators have a more developed sense of intuition.

Eventually, after days and months of daily practice, your sixth sense gets strong enough to work in concert with your material senses, so that during the day, as you go about your business, you're perceiving the world with a greater range of ability.

Developing your sense of intuition is truly one of the greatest gifts you can give yourself, all courtesy of the amazing power of meditation.

VISUALIZATION TO DEVELOP INTUITION

Here's a quick visualization you can do to help develop your intuition and strengthen your lazy "third" eye.

In a meditative state, imagine breathing in and out of your forehead. Just imagine that as you are inhaling, you are actually inhaling from your forehead and as you are exhaling you are exhaling from that same point.

Imagine you are in an ocean of white light and you are breathing that white light in and out of your forehead. As you breathe the light into your forehead, it fills your head and then your entire body with white light.

Continue doing this for a few minutes, just inhaling and exhaling white light into your body from your forehead. You may start to notice some light or patterns developing in your forehead. If you do, just allow them to be there and don't pay too much attention to them.

As you continue to breathe through your forehead, imagine that you have a large eye in the middle of your forehead that opens up and starts seeing. Imagine that this eye can clearly see your future and imagine your most perfect future, in the coming months and years.

Now feel that this eye that has opened up in your forehead is guiding you to your most perfect ideal life. Feel and affirm that throughout your day, every day, every step you make will be guided by this intuition toward creating the vision of your perfect life that you've just created.

Then just remain in that state of breathing white light into and out of your body from your forehead for as long as you like.

Using meditation to help free yourself from the confines of your senses and develop your intuition is so powerful and liberating.

But perhaps the greatest use of meditation for our purposes is when you combine it with very specific visualizations, you can use it to unblock and open your energy channels in order to raise your vibration and transition into higher, better worlds with higher, better versions of your life.

Content from this chapter is reprinted with permission from
Visualization For Weight Loss *by Jon Gabriel (Hay House, 2015).*

11

A SIMPLE VISUALIZATION TO RAISE YOUR VIBRATION

EXPERTS in energetic medicine tell us that 'where the mind goes the chi flows'. That is, when we bring our minds to any part of our bodies, the chi, or life-force energy, will be directed to that part of the body. When we use our imagination to visualize chi, in the form of white light going to a part of our body where there is an energy block, the chi acts like a kind of 'Drano', unblocking the energy channels.

Taoists have been using visualizations to open up their energy channels for thousands of years. Here's a meditation/visualization that I do, to unblock my energy channels and get my life-force energy flowing through my body.

It's based on Taoist meditations that I've been practicing since 1987.

- *Sit straight with your chin slightly down, so that your spine is like one long line from the bottom of your spine to the base of your head. Keep your mouth closed if possible and comfortable and let your tongue slightly touch the roof of your mouth. Have your hands gently folded together on your lap.*
- *Now take a deep breath in, and then let that breath out and*

relax. Just imagine there's a ball of light in your navel and it's circulating around. And it's getting brighter and brighter, and as it's circulating around it's pulling energy up from the earth. Energy is coming from the earth, into your feet, and into your shins and ankles, and into your calves, and into your knees, and it's circulating around your legs and your bones, and it's going into your thighs, and it's going into your pelvis, and it's going into that ball of energy in your navel.

- And as this ball is pulling energy up from the earth and spinning around your navel, imagine that it's also pulling energy down from the sky. That energy is filling your head with bright white light, and if you touch your tongue to the roof of your mouth, you might feel the trickle as that energy goes into your tongue and into your throat, filling your throat with bright white light. And you feel it move into your heart, filling your heart and your lungs with bright white light. And then down into your navel.

- So now your whole body is being filled with light. Energy from the earth is coming into your legs. Energy from the sky is coming into your head, and it is all meeting in your navel. And your navel is spinning around with bright white light, getting brighter and brighter and brighter. And this ball of white light is getting bigger and bigger so that it's filling your whole stomach and your pelvis and your thighs and your chest and your shoulders and your shins and your ankles and your head. It's getting bigger and bigger and brighter and brighter. And it's above your head and it's below your feet and you're covered in a big ball of bright white light. And every cell of your body is being bathed in this bright white light.

- Imagine the energy starting to move from one arm, into your hand and then into the other hand and up the other arm. So in this way, energy is flowing around your arms, as well. So now you have a ball of light in your navel that's circulating like a galaxy of light or a vortex. It's pulling energy up from the earth, into your legs and into the vortex. It's pulling energy *down from the sky, into your head and chest and into the energy vortex. Energy is also circulating around your arms, and your entire body is covered by an ever-growing ball of beautiful bright white light. Now just sit for a few minutes, with your back straight, your tongue lightly touching the roof of your mouth, and your hands folded together on your lap. Breathe into and out of your navel and imagine that while you breathe in, the spiral turns faster, like a pinwheel in the wind, and as you breathe out, the spiral turns faster, as well.*

- *Don't worry about which direction it turns, either clockwise or anti-clockwise is fine. you are circulating energy through your body. Just spend a few minutes breathing into and out of your navel and imagining the energy circulating and moving in all directions as you breathe. See the energy coming up from the earth, down from the sky, all converging in your navel and growing into an ever-brighter, ever-larger ball of energy.*

- *When you're ready to finish (you'll intuitively know this), imagine the vortex of light in your navel sucking up all the excess light that is coming up from the earth, down from the sky, and circulating all around your body. Imagine it all gets sucked into this circulating vortex and stored there as life-force vitality that you can use anytime you want or need.*

I practice a version of this every day, in the morning, usually for one to three hours.

When I'm done, I can feel my energy channels are open and flowing and I'm ready to start the day. I find a direct correlation between how well my energy channels are flowing in the meditation and how good the rest of my day will be. When my energy is flowing, my life is flowing. When my energy is blocked, my life is blocked.

After I've done the meditation, I know my energy channels are open and flowing and can handle the transmission of higher energies into and through my body to raise my vibration as high as possible. At that point I usually say the following to invite those higher energies in...

Higher self, higher loving energies and God, please totally occupy this body. Please speak through me, feel through me, act through me, and think through me, every minute of my life.

Please open up my energy channels and radiate your love and your light into this body and out into the world according to your will and your agenda, every minute of my life.

I surrender to you with all my heart and all my soul.

I surrender to this day.

After I say this, I feel an explosion of light go through my body and out into the world. Then I know that I am truly ready to start my day.

What I've come to know is that there are two components to being able to channel higher energies into your energy channels and through your body. One is you have to open the energy channels and that's exactly what a mediation like this is designed to do. And the other step is you have to ask those higher energies to come through you. There are lots of different names we've given those higher energies over the years, such as soul, spirit, higher self, God force, divine will, divine light, divine inspiration. All of these higher energies can flow into your body once your energy channels are open, but *they will only come in if you ask.*

I see these energies all as higher aspects of ourselves. Interacting with these energies intimately over the years, I've come to learn that they are collectively all conscious energies and they are very respectful of our personal freedom and our free will.

They will not assume anything.

You have to ask them to come in and work through you.

You may be wondering how you know if your energy channels are open or blocked. That's something you get better at knowing over time. As you imagine white light flowing through your body, you'll notice that in some areas of your body it's easier to imagine the light flowing than in others. In general, any part of your body that you can't easily imagine white light flowing to has some blockages.

Also you may not be able to imagine the light at all. That's OK; instead just feel your way through your body while you're meditating. Again, you will notice that some parts of your body you can feel your way through better than others. Maybe you can feel your awareness entering your chest and legs but not your stomach, for example. In that case you may want to spend more time imagining energy going into your stomach and continue trying to feel your way into and through your stomach area.

You may also experience a tingling sensation in parts of your body, a slight vibration, some mild pressure or heat in certain parts of your body. Or you may experience the feeling of a current of warm water passing through you or even the feeling of a mild electric current passing through you.

These sensations typically occur in time after you've had some experience and practice. If you feel any of these sensations in some parts of your body and not others, it's likely that the areas you can't feel are more blocked. Also if you try to scan your awareness through your entire body, from head to toe, and you notice that there's some parts of your body that are harder to bring your awareness to, it's likely that those areas are blocked.

You get better and better at feeling the subtle differences in your energy over time. Either way, a meditation like this can unblock your energy channels and keep them open and flowing on a daily basis.

Once your energy channels are open and that energy has the capacity to enter your body without harming you and then you ask these higher aspects of yourself to come in and work through you, you've done your part to form a divine partnership with your higher self. What happens after that can only be described as magical.

I believe that we are all channels for our higher selves and these higher energies, and our job in life, our purpose, is to do the work necessary to allow the higher energies to enter our bodies and work through us.

When that happens, we are truly living our life's purpose. You then become a divine instrument. You become a tool for the will of God. A clear channel to allow divinity to express itself in this world. Those higher energies will always guide you to the exact right places and situations where you can be of greatest service to life itself. And, of course, the higher energies will allow you to raise your vibration and transition to higher universes where life is more beautiful and loving and things just work out easier.

I rarely talk about meditation unless people ask, and I never tell people how long I meditate every day. Any time I tell people that I meditate two to three hours a day, the first thing they always say is, "Oh, I don't have time to meditate three hours a day." And I always nod, understandingly.

But in my mind, I'm thinking, "It's possible that maybe one of the reasons you don't have time to meditate three hours a day is because you don't meditate three hours a day."

I find that the more time I spend meditating, the more available time I have for the rest of my life. It's as if the calmness and flow you experience in your meditation spills over into your life. You experience fewer dramas and more synchronicities and find that things get done better, easier and quicker.

It seems pretty magical, but I've seen it happen time and again over a 30-plus-year period. It's as if we move to a universe where things just flow easier and everything seems to work out better. And in a very real sense that's EXACTLY what's happening.

When we don't meditate, our rational minds, with their limited perception and limited information, take over and our lives become frantic and chaotic. Sure, we're *busy* all the time, but that doesn't necessarily mean that we're productive. Most of the time we're just putting out fires all day long because our lives become a reflection of our chaotic and discordant, blocked energy. All this activity gives us the illusion of productivity, but in reality, very little actually gets accomplished because it's all so inefficient.

But when you meditate for long periods of time every day, everything flows in your life in a completely different way and you're incredibly more productive even though you're not that 'busy'. Life just opens up, time stands still and things somehow get done.

The Taoists have a book, the *Tao Te Ching*, that forms a basis for their whole approach to living. The opening line of verse 37 reads:

"The Tao does nothing, but leaves nothing undone."

It's this 'active non-action' I'm talking about when I talk about the flow of life that comes from open, flowing energy channels.

I wrote most of this book in a few weeks. It just kept coming out of me. Every time I sat to meditate, there was a voice in my head that was literally reading the book to me. And then when I was done meditating, I just transcribed everything that I just heard. It was almost like the book was created outside of time and was 'told' to me during meditation.

As we know, time is not real in a linear sense. The past didn't happen in the past and the future isn't going to happen in the future. We all exist in the eternal present, so it's safe to say that everything that ever will be created has been created already. Every song, book, poem, movie, invention or idea has already been created. All we do is channel the information. And the best way to channel information is – literally – to open your energy channels as much as possible. That's how information comes to us: through our energy channels.

When we meditate every day and consciously open our energy channels through visualizations like the one above, our channels are as open as possible and then we – literally – become channels for creativity.

In the 2019 movie *Yesterday*, the main character finds himself in an alternate universe, where The Beatles never existed. He then goes on to 'write' all the Beatles songs and become a world-famous composer. Now obviously he didn't write those songs, he didn't 'create' them. All he did was bring them over from one universe to another.

But it begs the question: did the Beatles write/create the Beatles' songs? I would suggest that since all time exists now, those songs were created before the Beatles were even born, or more specifically, at the same time – in the eternal present. All they did was channel the information. Like all creators, their inspiration came from their ability to channel the information into the world.

There's a well-known phenomenon in science called 'multiple discovery'.

Multiple discovery is when two or more people, that have no contact with each other, invent or discover the same thing at the same time. This happens quite frequently and has been happening since the dawn of time. Examples of multiple discovery include the formulation of calculus, by Isaac Newton, Gottfried Wilhelm Leibniz and others in the 17th century, the discovery of oxygen in the 18th century by Carl Wilhelm Scheele, Joseph Priestley, Antoine Lavoisier and others, the blast furnace, invented independently in China, Europe and Africa, and the crossbow, invented independently in China, Greece, Africa, Northern Canada and the Baltic countries.[1]

It appears to be happening with increased regularity, as Nobel Prizes are now routinely awarded to more than one person for the same discovery.

While this phenomenon has baffled scientists for centuries, it makes perfect sense when you consider the fact that all discoveries and inventions already exist outside of time and are available to anyone who can channel them.

It typically takes months and in many cases years to write a book. The majority of this book was written in a couple of weeks and it was simply because the inspiration was being channeled at a very rapid rate. It was worth every minute I invested in unblocking so that the book could flow through me.

When you meditate for long periods of time, you literally become inspired. The word inspired is from the Latin phrase *in spiritus*, which means letting spirit into your body. And that's exactly what you're doing when you meditate. The Greeks had another term, *entheousiasmos* – 'letting the God in' – from which we get our word 'enthusiasm'.

You literally become inspired and enthusiastic because you are allowing Spirit to come into your body. Our higher energies, our higher self, our soul, our spirit – whatever you want to call it and however you want to look at it – can only come into our bodies through our energy channels. And they can only come into our energy channels if those channels are open and flowing – and, even then, only if we can handle the higher vibrational transmission.

Creativity actually occurs outside of time, by our higher energies and it is then transmitted to us – perhaps through our Muses, the Spirits of Creativity. But the information can only come to us if the channels are open.

When those channels are blocked and higher energies can't enter, we become like chickens with their heads cut off, in a very real sense. We lose our sense of direction and therefore we have no direction. We're running around aimlessly and to no purpose. When our higher energies can't communicate with us, our rational mind takes over and the rational mind is a great servant but it's a merciless taskmaster. It was never meant to be in charge; it was always meant to take direction from our higher self.

When you meditate, things slow down. You have all the time you need. Everything happens with amazing synchronicities. And we're *inspired* to produce things *enthusiastically* that we didn't even know where we were capable of. It's paradoxical, but the more time you spend meditating, the more time you have available for the rest of your life.

Of course, when you're just starting you want to start slow. Practicing a visualization like this for 10 or 15 minutes a day in the beginning is great.

A meditation like this is a perfect place to start, but let's take it a step further. Let's combine these meditation and visualization techniques to not only open our energy channels but to travel, with intention, to the highest, most amazing worlds available to us...

Content from this chapter is reprinted with permission from
Visualization For Weight Loss *by Jon Gabriel (Hay House, 2015).*

12

CHOOSING THE UNIVERSE THAT'S RIGHT FOR YOU

BY CLEARING YOUR ENERGY CHANNELS, you can raise your vibration and rise higher in the ocean of universes. But let's see if we can take it a step further. Can we use our intention to not only travel to the highest universe possible but to also travel to the one that has the *exact* specific life we want in the *exact* specific world we'd like to live in?

For example, you may want to go to the universe where you win the lottery. Or maybe you want the universe where you get the perfect job or marry the perfect partner.

Sometimes, you want something very, very specific, and, of course, you're free to desire anything you like.

BUT there's a catch.

For years I used to visualize creating a *specific result*. And yes, after doing all the work of clearing my energy channels and meditating and dealing with my traumas and everything else, I learned that, yes, indeed, you can often get EXACTLY what you want.

But what you want might not exactly be the best-case scenario for you.

When I wrote my first book, *The Gabriel Method*, I wanted a specific publisher to publish it. Each morning I visualized that publisher publishing the book. After a few days a literary agent contacted me out of the blue and asked if he could represent me. He had just read the self-published version of the book and loved it. He mentioned he had close connections with the very publisher I wanted.

Of course, I said "Sure!", because this is *exactly* what I was visualizing. It was *exactly* what I wanted. That same publisher published the book and it did great. It was translated into 16 languages and sold in 60 countries and was a bestseller in three languages. At one time it was ranked number 10 of all books sold on the largest online platform.

But the reality is, it would have been much more profitable for me to continue to publish the book on my own. Because when I was publishing the book on my own, I was making $20 profit per book. This enabled me to advertise online and in 2009 I was Google's largest weight-loss advertiser.

But once I sold the rights to the publisher, I was only making $1 a book profit, so I no longer had enough money in the sale of the book to afford to advertise.

I didn't really think that one through fully, but, at the time, I wanted to do THAT SPECIFIC THING IN THAT SPECIFIC WAY, and no one could tell me otherwise.

I learned this lesson over and over for years. If I visualized getting a specific result, when I was in a deep state of meditation, I almost always could get it. But I also learned over and over that getting that *specific* result wasn't really what I wanted and didn't really make me any happier. Not only that but, more often than not, the whole thing backfired and even though I got the 'thing', something unforeseen would screw up everything.

Once I learned my lesson, I did things differently. Without focusing on any specific outcome, I focused *on the feeling* of what I wanted. Such as the feeling of tremendous success in my profession and the feeling of helping lots of people. In the example above, I did go on to experience both of those things. It just didn't happen specifically through the sale of the books. It happened through coaching and teaching and lecturing instead. So, I did get what I wanted, and I did get to a place where my universe matched my feeling, but in a more 'roundabout' way.

You see, your conscious, rational mind makes decisions based on the information at hand, not only what 'is' but what it believes 'can be' or 'ought to be'. Because of its limited perspective, it can't possibly think of everything, much less the 'optimal' scenario, which might not be visible at all from where you're standing right now.

The path to an 'optimal' universe might not be a straight line, but a twisty-turny one, full of things that are invisible around the corner. In retrospect, had I exercised more of my quantum sense, my intuitive mind, I might have shut up long enough to hear voices telling me, "You're going to be better off doing it *this* way instead. Let me show you, bit by bit, how to get you what you truly want." I might also have let go of assumptions about what would have been 'best' for me and attachments to specific outcomes that were anchoring me away from a whole bunch of fantastic universes waiting for me to experience them.

Faustian Bargains

It's not like there's a lack of myths, legends, fables and stories that warn us of exactly this very problem. That is, this trap of being overly specific – of wanting what you think you want from a limited perspective, and how this might be problematic. It's not like we haven't been warned, over and over and over again.

In the 1967 movie *Bedazzled* with Dudley Moore and Peter Cook, Dudley Moore plays Stanley Moon, a short-order cook who's obsessed with the waitress, Margaret, who works with him at Wimpy Burger. Peter Cook is the Devil. You can already see where this is going.

SPOILER ALERT!

Peter Cook made a bet with God. The first one to get 100 billion souls would 'win'. Dudley is potentially soul number 100 billion. The Devil offers Stanley the opportunity to have his dreams come true, if only he sells his soul to him, so Stanley agrees to the deal: his soul in exchange for the girl.

The Devil gives him seven chances, in seven different universes, in seven different timelines to try different lives with this girl. He's free to accept or reject each scenario, but after the seventh try, or at the end of the life that most works for him, whichever comes first, he has to give up his soul.

In one life, he's enormously rich and he marries her, but then she starts fooling around with the hired help. So that didn't work. In another life, he's a famous rock star and she's obsessed with him. But then another rock star comes along that she likes more. This more attractive rock star, hilariously played by the Devil, sang a song about how he doesn't love or need anyone, which made him irresistibly attractive.

When Stanley questioned the Devil about the 'coincidence' of the rock star's appearance looking just like the Devil, the Devil replies, "Well, there's a little bit of me in everyone."

Each time Stanley tries a different life, the Devil finds a way to screw him over.

So, finally, Stanley decides that it's not about being rich, it's not about being famous, he just wants a life where she is madly in love with him, "without the involvement of, or interference with, any other man", and that was his final chance.

In that life, in that universe she is indeed madly in love with him, but they were both women. Worse, they were both nuns and nothing can happen because "a love so pure couldn't be defiled by the flesh" or words to that effect. Basically, whatever Stanley tried, the Devil would somehow foil his plans. Which was, perhaps, the whole point.

Stanley was screwing *himself* over, and the Devil was merely taking advantage of the loopholes.

Because, in reality, Stanley didn't really want Margaret to love him. What he wanted was the "feeling" of being in love and the "feeling" of being loved back by the object of his desire. That's what he wanted. It didn't have to be with *her*, specifically, although it *might* have been. But fixating on a specific person and a specific outcome immediately closed Stanley off from a better outcome and, incidentally, blocked him off from a truly authentic relationship with Margaret, that took into account what she wanted too. But no one could tell Stanley otherwise. He had to learn for himself.

To see other takes on a similar theme, there are lots of stories like this. I strongly recommend the 1946 film *It's a Wonderful Life*, where the character, George, unwittingly makes a deal with God. It makes the same point as *Bedazzled*, but in a beautiful, heart-warming way.

I know there are techniques out there for traveling to the specific world and universe you want, to get a very specific outcome. One I've heard of is called Matrix Energetics. I've never used it and I can't comment on its effectiveness. Both my ex-wife and daughter have tried it and they were both effective at getting their desired result, but neither of them still use it for the same reasons we just discussed. The specific outcome didn't give them what they *really* wanted. They got what they were trying to get in a material sense, but they weren't happier and things weren't any better. In most cases they were worse. From a feeling perspective nothing changed. That's why I say you have to stick with focusing on the *feelings* of success.

It's All About the Feeling

I cannot overemphasize this crucial point.

When people 'want' something – the career, the lifestyle, the house, the partner – they nearly always focus on the specifics. This, on one level, is a perfectly reasonable thing to do. You see a picture of a glamorous career and lifestyle, the beautiful house or person and get a taste of how having that makes you feel and you think, "Oh, yeah baby, I'll have a piece of that!" because, after all, it's 'the piece of that' that made you feel what you felt, so, naturally, you have to get the 'pieces of that' to continue feeling that feeling.

But you can lose sight of the forest for the trees, stuck in the details, forgetting the big picture. You forget that the 'pieces' are only there to give you the *feeling, which is the real, energetic experience.*

To some extent, the 'pieces' are only paraphernalia, props to encourage a state of consciousness suffused with an uplifting, positive feeling of success – whatever 'uplifting' or 'positive' or 'success' might mean to you.

When you focus on the feeling of what you want, on the energy of what you want, you'll open yourself up to the universes that will resonate with your vibe, and you'll end up in a universe which *reinforces* those feelings.

The universe where you win the lottery may also be the universe where the world economy collapses or it may be the universe where (God forbid) your favorite pet dies, or worse.

You might be miserable in the universe where you marry so-and-so because you were actually 'meant' to marry someone else. You may be able to get the specific job you want but there's another universe where you invented something and made millions on that invention, but you're missing out on that because you used your intention to be in this reality.

There are an infinite number of unforeseen things that can happen when you switch universes, so you're really better off not being too specific.

When you use a technique to change some specific aspect of your life, by journeying to a universe that has that *one* thing you seek and you do so without changing the inherent quality of your energy, something's got to give.

You might get to a 'higher' universe, at least for a short while, but you won't be able to sustain it.

The universe you're in is *always* consistent with your 'energy/consciousness profile'.

Achieving a sustainable timeline in a sustainable universe requires a sustainable change of vibration, not simple tricks and techniques. Without raising your vibration, you're not really going to go to a higher universe, since your total energy profile will not be consistent with that higher universe. Instead you'll be going to a universe with a similar vibrational frequency and just *some* of the aspects of your life will have been moved around – and it's usually the most superficial aspects of that universe.

It's like moving around the chairs on the deck of an ocean liner. It's the same ocean liner, going to the same place, just a different seating arrangement.

It's like putting on the same play with different actors and backdrop scenery; even a change of script won't work in some cases. You might fool yourself into thinking it's a different play for a while, but *Richard III* is still *Richard III* whether it's Laurence Olivier in medieval garb, Ian McKellen in a pseudo Nazi uniform or Kevin Spacey as it's been reimagined in *House of Cards*.

Your soap opera life will still be a soap opera, whether you're in the U.K. and it's called *Coronation Street*, in the U.S. and it's called *Days of Our Lives* or if you're in Mexico and it's called *Cuna de Lobos*.

They're all different, but they're all the same too.

Of course, if you like where your ship is going, if you like stories about megalomaniacs or if you like stories about people endlessly creating dramas for themselves, that's your right.

But if you want something different, and if you're really serious about it, the best-case scenario is to focus on transitioning into a universe where you're truly uplifted – happy, healthy, vibrant, energetic, passionate, loved, in love, productive, successful and living your life's purpose, without focusing on the *specifics* of how that would look.

So how do you get into THAT realm of universes?

You focus on the *feelings*. Then let the higher vibrations of those higher feelings, transition you into a higher universe that vibrates at a similar frequency.

Because that's what vibrations do, they move to an environment that matches their frequency. Look at a hot-air balloon, for example – when you heat the air inside the balloon, the vibration of the air molecules rises and then the balloon will rise until the air outside the balloon has the same vibrational frequency as the air inside the balloon.

It won't rise any higher, unless you heat the air some more and it won't fall any lower unless you cool the air. The balloon will always float at a level where the inner density is the same as the outer density – where the outside vibration of the atmosphere matches the vibration of the air inside the balloon.

In the same way, we will always dwell in a universe and in a situation where the outside vibration of the universe matches our 'inner', personal vibration.

As I mentioned before, there are reasons why we might want to consciously or unconsciously be in a lower vibrational existence, but for the most part, if you raise your vibration, you will move to a higher universe and situation that matches that vibration.

How would you feel if you were truly uplifted?

Generating the Feeling

The common objection to the 'feeling first' worldview is that people say, "It's hard to 'feel' a particular way when I look at my life, which is full of stuff I don't want, and it all sucks a big wiener."

I hear you...

Generating the feeling is another underutilized birthright. But generating the feeling is a quantum talent. It looks beyond the material world into the realm of the non-material. 'Feelings' are vibrations, wave energies that only 'coalesce' when we direct our attention in that direction.

Once again, 'where the mind goes, energy flows'. And, once again, this is where we have to use our birthright of imagination and visualization to 'create' an experience that 'isn't there yet'.

So, let's take a moment to practice feeling our desired outcome...

Try generating these feelings one at a time.

How does it feel to be:

- Happy
- Healthy
- Vibrant
- Energetic
- Passionate
- Loved
- In love
- Productive
- Successful
- Rich
- Abundant
- Living your life's purpose
- Healing the world and others?

Each one of these feelings has a certain vibrational frequency.

In meditation you can focus on the feelings of these emotional states and the corresponding vibration that accompanies these feelings.

Then, while in the meditative state, fill your body with these feelings. Imagine your body is vibrating at the frequency of these feelings.

Then, while still in that vibrational state, imagine that you are floating up, like a hot-air balloon, from one universe to the next until you arrive at the universe that matches this vibrational frequency.

Best universe possible meditation/visualization technique:

Here's an example of a live guided meditation/visualization that takes you to the universe that matches the feelings you create. This to me is the ideal technique to practice to consciously transition to higher universes in the best way possible. I recommend practicing this meditation every morning. It's simply an expanded version of the meditation exercises that we talked about earlier for opening up your energy channels.

This meditation was performed live at The Omega Center in New York, August 2019 eomega.org

To listen to a recording of this visualization visit thegabrielmethod.com/bestworld

- *So, just sitting comfortably.*
- *Take a deep breath in. Take a deep breath out of your mouth.*
- *I'd like you to imagine there's a ball of beautiful, bright white healing light circulating around your navel. It's like a whirlpool of light, maybe the size of a softball or a volleyball. It doesn't really matter. And it's just spinning around, circulating around your navel, getting brighter and brighter and brighter. It's like a whirlpool of light or a galaxy of light. You're just breathing into it. If you can imagine each time you breathe in it spins more like a pendulum in the wind.*
- *You breathe in, it spins out more. You breathe out and it spins more. And it's just circulating around your navel getting brighter and brighter and brighter. And you can imagine also that energy as it's circulating around your navel, it's pulling energy up from the earth.*
- *It's pulling energy around. It's pulling earth energy into your feet, and into your knees, and into your legs, and your thighs. In whatever way you want to conceptualize it. It's pulling energy into this ball of light in your navel.*
- *So you've got this beautiful bright ball of light in your navel and you're pulling energy up from the earth into it and it's getting brighter and brighter. You can imagine as you're breathing into this ball of light in your navel and as it's circulating around getting brighter and brighter, and as it's pulling energy up from the earth into it, you're also pulling energy down from the sky into the top of your head.*

- *If you touch your tongue to the top of your mouth, the roof of your mouth, you can imagine that energy you might even feel a trickle of that energy going into your tongue, and into your throat, into your heart, and into the ball of light in your navel.*

- *So you have this ball of light circulating around and getting brighter and brighter, pulling energy up from the earth. It's pulling energy down from the sky. It's all mixing like the yin and yang, heaven and earth thing, and as it's doing that, it's getting brighter and brighter. You may want to even bring in your creative energy, your sexual energy into the ball of light in your navel as well. You can bring it into there and it's all mixing together to create an amazing chi. Earth energy, heaven energy, life-force energy, circulating around getting powerful and brighter. Raising your vibration, almost like a fire in a hot-air balloon. Raising your vibration. Your whole body.*

- *As you're sitting there with this ball of light in your navel, pulling energy up from the earth, down from the sky, bringing your life-force creative energy into it. Getting brighter and brighter, I'd like you to imagine that you're also in an infinite ocean of beautiful, bright white healing light. Maybe you can't see it with your eyes, but it's there. You can feel it, so bright. So powerful. So healing. Every particle that this light touches it heals. Every cell, it heals. Every particle that it touches, it raises your vibration to a higher frequency.*

- *And it's just bathing, just bathing us in that infinite ocean. And as you're sitting there with this ball of beautiful bright white healing light circulating around your navel, pulling energy up from the earth, down from the sky. Pulling your creative life-force energy into it, making it like a furnace, a powerful engine. And in this ocean of beautiful, bright white light, I'd like you to imagine that the pores of your skin open up and all of this beautiful, bright white healing light comes rushing into your body, filling your body with light. So every cell of your body, you can feel it rushing into your arms and your legs, can feel it rushing into your heart and your chest, your digestive system, your kidneys and liver, spleen and gallbladder. You can feel it in your eyes, and your face, and your tongue.*

- *You can feel it going up your spine and your legs, your whole body is glowing with this energy. So you've got this ball of light in your navel spinning around, getting brighter and brighter. It's pulling energy up from the earth. It's pulling energy down from the sky. You got your creative life-force energy in there, making it stronger. You're in this ocean of beautiful, bright white light. Pores of your skin have opened up. Every particle of your body is vibrating at the same frequency as that light. So your DNA is changing. Your DNA is being activated to be the highest vibration of your core self.*

- *The core of your bones is being rejuvenated in this glowing light of life-force vitality. The life-force vitality that you had as a kid is being renewed. So, your body is just becoming younger and more powerful. And you're in this ocean of beautiful, bright white light and every cell of your body is vibrating at the frequency of this beautiful, bright white light, like the switch, the dimmer switch on a light. As you can turn the dimmer switch on a light and make it brighter and brighter, I'd like you to imagine that you're turning the dimmer switch on the light of this ocean of energy and it's getting brighter and brighter. So you're turning it and you can see and feel it getting brighter and lighter at a higher frequency. And as that's happening, every cell of your body is vibrating at a higher frequency. All your energy channels are open and flowing, and you're just light.*

- *And so now you're vibrating at a higher frequency. And so you can turn this dimmer switch brighter and brighter. And as you're doing it, your bones start to glow brighter and brighter. Your skin, the cells, your DNA, everything glows at a higher frequency.*

- *And as you're glowing at a higher frequency, you can imagine*

that every cell in your body is being infused with the vibration
of positive physical and emotional states. Feel every cell of
your body being infused with the vibration of happiness.

- Now that you're here, you can give this light, beautiful energy
different flavors. Play with this, joyfully. Imagine every cell of
your body resonating at the frequency of each of these feelings,
one at a time…

- Health

- Vibrance

- Passion

- Love

- Being in Love

- Success

- Living Your Life's Purpose

- Feel your energy rising higher and higher and feel every cell of
your body resonating at the vibrational frequency of these
positive states. And as you're doing that, you can imagine that
because your vibration is getting higher, you're drifting higher
and higher to more pleasant realities. More pleasant versions
of this universe.

- Like a balloon in the middle of the ocean, you're rising higher
and higher. Your bones are glowing at a higher and higher
frequency and you're moving higher and higher to universes
that match your frequency. And you can see it happening very
quickly. You're moving from one life to another, from one
universe to another. The highest, most positive universe for
you, where things are flowing beautifully and effortlessly, your
energy is flowing through your body beautifully and
effortlessly and your life is flowing. Things are happening
easier, faster, quicker. People are kinder. The universe may be a
little bit cleaner, a little bit safer, a little more pure. Maybe
there's a chance some really amazing things will happen to
heal the world.

- You can see yourself in that universe. It looks and feels just
like this universe. It's just a little bit different, it's a little bit

better. Maybe whatever you work on professionally is happening just a little easier. You can imagine that you're in this universe where whatever you're working on when you go back to your life, it's just a little easier. The sales happen a little quicker. The deal closes quicker. The relationships happen, things happen easier, just a little bit smoother and you're just vibrating at a higher and higher frequency. Just feel that. Just take a moment and just be quiet in your own time space to feel what it feels like to be in a higher frequency existence, a higher energy universe. And so maintain that and feel that. A place where everything's flowing and magical. Just feel that feeling. Whatever it feels like for you, just connect with it.

- *Then, just in your own time and space, I'd like you to imagine that all that energy from that universe, that ocean of energy, comes into that beautiful ball of light in your navel. It's like you bring it all in and you keep it in you. You keep the energy from a higher reality where everything's beautiful and pleasant, and smooth. Keep the energy inside you. It all goes into the ball of light in your navel and you store it there. You store it in your navel so it's like a furnace of high vibrational energy that you could use for vitality, for inspiration, for power, and to excel in every aspect of life. You just store it all there as your personal storehouse of power, vitality, vibration. You connect with it and allow it to guide you to the highest and most beautiful reality possible. In your own time and space open your eyes...*

If you practice a meditation like this every morning, you'll be amazed at how your life changes over time. And my experience is that it changes at an exponential rate. It's almost like being a billionaire. If you look at Bill Gates, maybe it took him five years to make his first million. But now he probably makes a million dollars an hour! That's not an exaggeration by the way. If you make $8.7 billion a year, that equals a million dollars an hour.

If you practice a meditation like this for ten years, you might be able to accomplish more in one day, in terms of success in transitioning to higher universes, than you might have accomplished in two years, when you first started. The progress and success at this level grows like compound interest, at an exponential rate. Your ability to get into deeper states while meditating, to open your energy channels, to energize your body, to visualize success – these abilities are very much like a muscle that gets stronger with use. I can't encourage you strongly enough to make a practice like this a daily habit, preferably first thing in the morning.

The key is:

NEVER MISS A DAY

The people that make real progress in meditation are the ones that swear by it and do it every morning, or evening, without fail – the ones who are hooked and addicted to it. And usually when you look at their lives, they have a kind of flow and balance and prosperity in them that most lives don't. I have a friend who's been meditating for at least 35 years. He lives a simple life and works as a lawyer for the U.S. Government in Washington D.C. He makes a pretty good government salary. The whole time he's been working for the government he's been buying properties all around the D.C. area. He's worth tens of millions of dollars. But he still keeps his job with the government. He likes people, he likes going to work every day. He travels a lot and he lives a very simple, low-stress life. He has amazing inner experiences and his eyes really light up if you can get him to share some of those experiences. But his outside life is simple, prosperous and drama-free. He also never misses a day of meditating. He's floating in the ocean at just the level he wants to be, right now.

It's All for the Now

There's a paradox here. Even though you're meditating and strengthening your ability to generate feelings for a 'future universe', the generation of feeling is always *in the now* and *for the now*.

You have to meditate for the calmness and joy and higher vibration that the practice gives you in the moment, in the now, not because "someday it's all going to come together". If you meditate for 'someday', you can easily get frustrated and discouraged if things are not happening quickly enough – if you're not reaching the 'goal' quick enough, if your new universe hasn't 'arrived yet'.

If the actual meditation that you are experiencing is, in and of itself, the goal, if the feelings are, in and of themselves, the goal, there's nothing to be frustrated about. That's the way it is for me at this point. My meditation is very much the enjoyment of my life and the part of my day I relish the most.

The experience is its own reward.

Moving to a better 'neighborhood of universes', and all the other fringe benefits that we've talked about all throughout this book is just an inevitable side effect.

I would encourage you to form the daily habit of practicing a meditation like this. Get hooked, get addicted to it, enjoy the moment and let all the other fringe benefits accrue behind the scenes, at their own pace and in their own time, without you putting too much 'thinking' into it or trying to 'second guess' what might happen.

Leave yourself open for surprises.

I always say to my daughter, "Nourish yourself each day and things will work out in the best way possible." It's a huge paradigm shift and it's taken me years of learning and unlearning to get here but I know it's true. If you nourish yourself with a mediation like this every day, things will always work out in the best way possible, because you'll always be in the highest vibration you can be in, which means you'll be living in the most ideal world, and most perfect life scenario.

13

SEVERING THE CORDS THAT HOLD US DOWN

A BELIEF CAN BE DEFINED as a 'thought that you keep thinking, regardless of any evidence for or against that thought'. Since belief is often independent of 'evidence', you're free to believe whatever you want. And, like everything else, there are beliefs that are 'negative' or 'positive'.

For me, 'negative' means 'limiting', 'constricting' or even 'blinding'.

The tendency to think negative, limiting beliefs is common – dismayingly common. So much so that we can take them for granted and tend to dismiss the power of these thoughts, and we're barely conscious of the negative paths the mind travels on a daily basis.

But our minds are powerful and determine how we create the experience of our reality. We already know the universe as we 'see' it is very different to the way it really is, and our experience of reality affects what our minds 'believe', but our beliefs also affect what our minds choose when they create this illusory world we experience.

Researchers have observed how thoughts become reality in medical studies and in the context of different cultures.

Ever heard of the word 'placebo'? It means a substance that has no objective effect on an illness. And yet there's a 'placebo effect', where you believe something can cause healing.

But have you ever heard of the term 'nocebo'? The nocebo effect is when you believe something negative will happen, and it comes to pass. Anthropologists first observed this in cultures where shamans would place curses. Having resided in Australia for 10 years, I know about research documenting indigenous medicine men in Australia performing a curse called 'pointing the bone'. If they aimed a sharpened kangaroo bone at a tribe member, that member believed so strongly in the curse that they would soon sicken, stop eating and drinking, wither, and eventually die unless a healer intervened – a self-fulfilling prophecy of death based on belief.[1]In another example about the power of negative beliefs, we turn to Deepak Chopra – international best-selling author on spirituality. Chopra often references the story of a friend who went in to see a doctor, and, as part of a general screening, the doctor ordered a lung X-ray.

When the images came back, the doctor found a spot and brought the patient back in for a follow-up. "I have some bad news," the doctor told the patient. "You have lung cancer, and you have just a few months to live."

Within a few months, the man passed away as the doctor had predicted. When Chopra was going through his friend's belongings, he found a lung X-ray from 25 years earlier. When Chopra held it up to the light, he saw that the exact same spot was there.

The patient had lived with this spot in his lung for 25 years; it wasn't until someone told him that it was cancer that it actually became deadly.[2]

Our beliefs are a tool – a quantum tool.

They transcend material reality and material evidence, and they act as reality 'filters'. When they're negative, they cause us to see and experience unfortunate events. They are resistant to material evidence because their very nature prevents us from seeing and experiencing other realities – positive things – that would otherwise come easily to us if we had different filters in place.

We travel through universes all the time, whether we 'believe' in the principle or not. But at the most basic and fundamental 'belief level', our beliefs determine where in the multiverse we float.

When traveling through universes, we're simply not going to transition to a universe where we experience some positive event, if we don't believe that positive event is possible. Alternatively, we *might* believe the positive event is *possible but only on the condition* that we have to first work *really hard* to attain it.

Whatever we believe, the filter will exclude other possibilities so that the timeline we experience is consistent with our total energy profile – and that includes our beliefs. So it's the case that every timeline we experience is going to be entirely consistent with the totality of our beliefs, even if the result is that we'll just keep making our lives more and more difficult as the 'price to pay' before we allow ourselves to experience the desired result.

Most of these limiting beliefs are unconscious. We acquired them when we were young and impressionable. Someone may have made an off-handed comment like "life is hard", and the filter only let 'life is hard' universes match up with us. We accepted this as 'fact' and we adopted and accepted that view and it has been plaguing us ever since.

But the opposite is also true.

A chance positive comment when we're young and impressionable can make all the difference for the rest of our lives. I once heard of a lady who was poor growing up. When she was a young child, she came home from school one day and said to her mom, "Guess what? I just took an aptitude test and it said I could make a good telephone operator" (for the millennials – that's a human Siri). Her mom replied, "That's great honey, maybe one day you'll own the telephone company." She grew up to be a self-made billionaire. She attributes her success to the encouragement her mom gave her growing up.

One can't help but wonder what would have happened if her mom had instead said something like, "It's not that easy to be a phone operator. What makes you think you could actually do something like that?"

Negative programming is, unfortunately, what most of us receive at some point in our lives. Some of us get more, some of us get less. Some of us are more resilient to it, some of us less so. The result is that it just passes trauma and hardship down the line from one generation to the next. To me, this negative programming is a form of child abuse.

It's *usually* well intentioned. We say things to ourselves like, "We need to teach our kids that it's mean and cruel out there. Life's hard. We need to toughen them up. It's better they learn it now." But the reality is that when you teach a kid that life is hard, you've just programmed that reality into their brains.

The reality is that life isn't ultimately 'hard' or 'easy'. Life is an illusion – a well-constructed and utterly convincing illusion, but it's an illusion, nonetheless.

It's like a virtual reality game and we either know how to play it or we don't. Anything is possible and anything can either be hard or easy depending on whether you know the rules or not, or how much practice you get.

There is a version of us experiencing every conceivable reality in this very moment. It's up to us to access the reality that is most desirable for us, a universe that is consistent with where we are at.

So, one of the ways to make life easier is to change the settings on the game, change our filters. To do that we have to learn how to reprogram negative beliefs and how to create positive beliefs.

'Reprogramming the mind' is one of the most worthwhile things you can do, and it starts with *consciously* reprogramming your beliefs.

Your energy channels may be open and you have the energy and vitality to transition to the highest most beautiful universe, *but if you don't believe you're worthy of experiencing* that level of joy, *happiness or success*, your beliefs will stop you from fully transitioning into that universe.

If you feel you haven't 'worked hard enough' or 'suffered enough' or 'given enough', you won't get there. If you feel you haven't in some way 'earned' it, you won't get there.

Or if you think you're the type of person that 'doesn't have that kind of luck', well then, you'll filter out the universes that are 'only for the lucky'. But you're just creating that negative reality experience for yourself and your beliefs are keeping you and will continue to keep you in universes where you are suffering unnecessarily. The belief becomes like a tether to a hot-air balloon. It keeps you anchored to a lower vibrational universe.

Reprogramming negative beliefs can also help you open your energy channels and channel higher energies into your body.

As we've talked about, stress, trauma and emotional pain can all cause blockages in your energy channels. All of these experiences can contribute to the formation of negative beliefs.

When you change your beliefs, you can sometimes instantly change your emotional state and eliminate stress and emotional pain in minutes.

Eliminating negative beliefs and replacing them with positive, more functional beliefs is like finally disengaging the parking brakes or taking the tethers off of a hot-air balloon and allowing it to soar.

CHANGE YOUR BELIEFS AND YOU INSTANTLY CHANGE YOUR EMOTIONAL EXPERIENCE

Imagine this scenario: You're sitting at a lovely outdoor café in a downtown plaza on a Sunday. You're waiting for your spouse to meet you for lunch. You've both been running errands and planned to meet up at one o'clock. She's running a few minutes late, but it's such a beautiful day that you don't mind.

However, 10 minutes turns into 20 and then into 30 minutes.

Now you're beginning to get bothered. After all, your time is important and you have more errands to run; it's a little odd that she would keep you waiting. More than odd, it's a little rude.

Now she's 45 minutes late. The waiter comes by for the *fifth* time and asks again if you want to order. You say "no" and you feel your face flush. You're growing furious. You think of all the times she's been late, all the times she's disregarded your feelings. This is so inconsiderate. She must think she's more important than me, you say to yourself. Your negative emotions churn, your stress climbs, your stress hormones surge.

Finally, *finally*, you catch sight of her across the street. She waves as she spots you, comes over, and plops down with a laugh. She grabs the menu and orders a drink when the waiter comes by. You're practically in shock, you're so angry. You're tight and short with her. She can't even bother to apologize? She looks up from the menu and sees your expression. "What's wrong, dear?" she asks.

"What's wrong?" you blurt. "I've been here for an hour! You think you can just show up without apologizing or giving me an explanation?"

She stops, looks at her watch, and replies, "I'm not late; I'm right on time. It's one o'clock right now. Daylight saving time ended last night, and we moved the clocks forward. Oh, my darling, did you forget to reset your watch?"

In a moment, your emotional world has flipped. You feel a wave of relief wash over you as all your negative beliefs do a 180-degree turn. Your entire emotional chemistry is altered in this moment as well. Your negative thoughts are vaporized, and levels of stress hormones plummet as you realize, "She *does* care about my time. She *is* considerate of my feelings."

What changed? Your underlying beliefs surrounding the situation.

You were operating under the *false* notion that she was late, and that was causing a cascade of negative thoughts and opinions. The second that the belief changed all the negativity vanished because you realized that she was not at fault; *you* were at fault.

Change your beliefs, and you instantly change the thoughts, emotions and chemistry surrounding the issue.

Now imagine the same scenario, except there's no time change. Your spouse really is more than an hour late, and you're sitting at the table fuming. Your blood is boiling, your stress hormones are flowing, and you're inflamed emotionally and physically. She sits down, and you ask her in a voice that's quaking with anger, "How could you keep me waiting so long?"

She smiles and drops a brand-new set of car keys on the table. "Your birthday is tomorrow, and I just finished signing the papers on that BMW you wanted. It just took a little longer than I thought it would. Sorry about that… Happy birthday!"

How do you feel now?

The reality is that this time, instead of relief, you actually feel a wave of positive emotions wash over you. You feel your spouse's love and thoughtfulness. You feel warm – not inflamed – and you marvel at how lucky you are to be married to your spouse. You feel happy, secure, and content. This time, not only has all the negativity disappeared, it has been magically transformed to positive emotions of love, happiness, security, and joy. Again, in an instant, you've dramatically altered the flow of chemicals in your body, and it's all based on your beliefs. Change your beliefs, and you instantly transform your emotional state.

Here are a few good ways to eliminate negative beliefs and replace them with positive beliefs.

1) Saying affirmations while meditating. When you're meditating your mind is more powerful and your concentration is more focused. For this reason, saying affirmations while you meditate is extremely effective. I like to imagine every cell of my body saying the affirmations. Try this: While meditating, imagine every cell of your body saying positive affirmations like:

- Life is easy
- Life is an illusion
- I can effortlessly experience anything I want
- I effortless transition into the highest universe possible
- Good things easily come to me
- I am in an ocean of success
- Success is my birthright
- Success is my nature
- I effortlessly experience success in every aspect of my life
- I am safe

- Life is safe
- I am guided by my higher self/soul/God
- Time is an illusion
- I am immortal and eternal
- I am on an exciting adventure
- I am a universe traveler
- Life is fun
- Life is safe
- Life is exciting
- Life is an amazing journey
- I am loved
- I am lovable
- I feel love radiating through my body and out into the world
- My energy channels are open and flowing
- Higher energies easily flow into me and through me, allowing me to create anything I like
- I forgive myself
- I forgive life
- I am at peace with life
- I am one with my higher self
- I am living my life's purpose
- All day, every day, I am traveling to higher more beautiful universes, without having to even think about it.

And don't just say these affirmations. Feel the vibration in every particle of your being. Imagine every cell of your body saying them in concert, over and over again. Live them in your imagination as if they are *already* true. See yourself and *feel* yourself from the inside behaving in ways that are completely consistent with the affirmations, from the viewpoint that the reality has *already* happened.

2) Other ways to change dysfunctional beliefs:

- Subliminal success tapes – subliminal messages are also a great way to reprogram negative beliefs. The key with these is repetition. Try to listen to your favorite ones over and over for a while until you see evidence in your thinking and behavior that your beliefs are changing.
- Hypnotherapy – a good hypnotherapist can help you identify dysfunctional beliefs and reprogram them
- Using affirmations while doing meridian tapping or other mind–body techniques.

There are many other techniques out there to change limiting beliefs. But either way, however you do it, changing them is essential. When you eliminate the beliefs that bind you to a lower vibrational existence, it's like cutting the cords on that proverbial hot-air balloon, allowing you to soar to worlds and universes where you're experiencing the happiness, love, prosperity and success you desire.

Another way to open up your energy channels and raise your vibration is with sex. Here I go talking about my favorite topic again, ha ha!

But it has to be *conscious* sex, where you're using these same meditation and visualization techniques to move energy through you and your partner. If it's not conscious sex, it can be very damaging because it dissipates your energy and causes energy blocks. Done right, it can open worlds.

Content from this chapter is reprinted with permission from Visualization For Weight Loss *by Jon Gabriel (Hay House, 2015).*

14

TAPPING INTO YOUR MOST POWERFUL ENERGY

NOTE THIS CHAPTER CONTAINS EXPLICIT SEXUAL CONTENT.

I want to talk about sexual energy because sexual energy is an energy – a vitality. It's actually our most powerful creative life-affirming force. Just like everything is a vibration, everything is an energy: thoughts, emotions, life-force vitality, the physical body are all vibrations, they are all energies. And one of the most powerful types of energy is our sexual energy – the seat of our creative life force.

Taoists and many Eastern meditation masters have been studying sexual energy for thousands of years. And what I've learned is that conserving and cultivating your sexual energy, rather than dissipating it, is the secret to health, youth, vitality, strength, power, and vibration. You will be at your highest vibration possible when you are cultivating your sexual energy as opposed to dissipating it.

Sexual energy works differently for men and for women. Let's talk about men first.

The Dark Side and the Light Side of Male Sexual Energy

According to the Taoist system of sexual energy cultivation, the male body takes all the best energies that it has, and it brings it down into the sexual organs and it is infused into our sperm, to maximize the success of the reproductive process.

What happens when we have sex is that we dissipate that energy. And then, once we dissipate that energy, that energy is gone. And then our body goes into the process of taking all our best energy once again, bringing it down to our sexual organs, infusing our sperm with it, and then we dissipate it again.

Most men are dissipating their sexual energy all the time, without knowing it, without realizing that there's anything wrong and or bad about that.

But when we do this, it keeps our vibration lower. Each time we dissipate, our vibration gets lower and we get into this process where our body becomes like a sperm-production factory, constantly taking our best, most vital energy and infusing it into our sperm and then dissipating it. And the whole time our energy is getting lower and lower. We're getting more tired, and weaker, more dissipated.

This is our most vital, creative force that we can use to create, manifest, bring anything that we want into our world, and we're dissipating it. So rather than dissipating it, what you want to do is learn how to recycle that energy and bring it back into your body.

What most schools that teach the cultivation of sexual energy will tell you is that there's a difference between an orgasm and an ejaculation.

And you can learn through time and practice and exercises to separate an orgasm from an ejaculation. And when you do that, you can make love, have an orgasm, and not lose the energy. It can go back into your body and you can use it to strengthen your bones and organs, so you continue to vibrate at a very high frequency.

One key component in conserving sexual energy is that your energy channels have to be open and flowing. I'm sure you're beginning to see a pattern here – it's all about having your energy channels open and flowing. The key to success in nearly every aspect of life and in this case your sexual health and vitality is having your channels open.

The energy needs some place to go. If the channels are not open, your body will force you to expend that energy through the 'funnel' of ejaculation.

Also, an important thing about ejaculation is that the more often you release sperm, the more your body produces it. Once your body produces it, it then wants to release it again. So, it's actually harder to stop your body from ejaculating when you are ejaculating frequently.

In a way, it's very similar to breast milk. If a mother is nursing all the time, her body is producing milk continually. Once the milk ducts are full, the body will want to expel that milk.

But once the child is weaned, after a few days or in some cases weeks, the body stops producing the breast milk and the mother doesn't feel the need to breastfeed anymore. But the first couple of days is really difficult because there's a build-up of breast milk, and the body is pushing her to expel the breast milk.

After a month, two months, three months, it's not an effort anymore because the body's not producing the breast milk anymore and it's not getting backed up.

It's the exact same thing with sperm. If you're emitting sperm all the time, your body's going to be producing it. And when you ejaculate again, your body continues the cycle of production/ejaculation/dissipation.

In essence you become a factory of energetic dissipation, where you're constantly lowering your energy. Sex becomes like a drug or a hit. And you're continually looking for the next hit, either from yourself or from someone else. If you ever wonder why you don't have the energy to create, to start your own business, to excel in business, to work out, it could well be because you're releasing too much of this energy, through dissipation.

As the French author Honoré de Balzac said after making love to his mistress, "There goes another novel!" Nikola Tesla, possibly the greatest inventor of the 20th century, was known to say that "an inventor can't afford to lose that energy". UK prime minister Winston Churchill said that he didn't "lose his essence in bed". The French have aptly named an ejaculation *"La petite mort"* – the little death.

When we're ejaculating on a regular basis, sooner rather than later we become addicted to dissipating without knowing it.

When you're frequently dissipating your sexual energy, your consciousness goes into a lower state too. You go into a primal, survival state of consciousness where you're constantly looking for the right mate or trying to defend the one you have.

Other men become a threat. And you feel the need to 'control' your woman.

The perfect example to me of what it's like to be in that possessive, defensive state is the mating of the elephant seal.

Elephant seals are three-ton animals. They can barely move on the beach. During mating season all the females gather on the beach, and then the males fight for the right to mate with the females. But only one male is 'allowed to' mate with all the females.

Only one 'alpha male' wins the 'right to sex joust'.

Then that alpha male spends all his time trying to have sex with 40, 60, 100 females. But at the same time that he's on one side of the beach having sex with one seal, there's another male on the other end of the beach about to have sex with another female, even though, as a beta male, he's not 'supposed to'.

Now the dominant male has to hurry up and finish having sex. And then he's got to take his three-ton body to the other side of the beach and try to get there before the subordinate male is finished, to fight him off.

So, the dominant male is spending all his time and energy dissipating his sexual energy through sex, fighting to defend that right, and fighting to stop everyone else from having sex with his herd.

The irony is that for all the jousting of the males and the trophy of being alpha, the female elephant seals are actually pregnant from the year before and they give birth a relatively short time after the alpha mates with them. The alpha, exhausted from constantly trying to 'get his end in' and fighting off the other males, stops mating.

The females meanwhile resume hunting to keep milk production up for their newborns. The other males take the opportunity to frolic with the females and impregnate them for next year. The alpha is basically a cuckold stooge for the seal pod, completely oblivious to the reality going on all around him. It's all for nothing.

That is the exact state of consciousness that we live in when we're in this dissipating, addictive, confrontative, low-energy state. Everyone becomes a threat. Everyone either becomes a target – someone that we can hit on, or potentially prey on – or a threat: someone that's threatening what we have. We are living under siege in a scarcity, a low-energy state of consciousness.

When we're in a low-energy, low-consciousness state we're reframing everything negatively, with constant negative thoughts producing feelings of stress. The stress is blocking our energy channels and we start to become denser. The combination of blocked energy channels and the constant negative, fearful thoughts causes us to become denser and denser.

This low-energy, low-consciousness place is taking us out of a higher-consciousness state where we can come up with creative solutions for our life, creative solutions for our jobs, creative solutions for our careers, creative solutions for our relationships.

The vicious cycle of lower and lower consciousness leads us into lower and lower universes and timelines because our vibrations are always getting lower and lower. And it's all because we are in an addictive, energy-dissipating state.

But when you break the vicious cycle of dissipation and learn to conserve your sexual energy, then you are no longer in that 'headspace', or 'groinspace'. You are no longer in an addictive place, needing your addictive hit. When you break the cycle, there's no longer any interest in ejaculating.

While it might be tricky in the beginning to break the cycle, after a certain period, not dissipating becomes the easiest thing in the world. You cannot even imagine ejaculating. You're no longer addicted. You're no longer dissipating and you're no longer feeling threatened.

And you can have an amazing sex life because the orgasms that you have are more profound. They're much better than what you have from just ejaculating. They fill your whole body. Having reversed the cycle, you're filling your whole body with vitality.

The vicious cycle becomes a creative and generative cycle. Over time you just naturally resonate at higher and higher vibrations and you float to a higher and higher universe because you are not dissipating anymore. You're in a relaxed, creative, powerful place where you're getting higher and higher energy.

One thing I will say is be patient with yourself. Breaking the cycle is not always easy.

But I can tell you that being aware of what's going on is so liberating because you have a way to get out of it. You have a way to pull yourself up by the bootstraps and get out of a life of slow dissipation. And when you do, it's pretty amazing.

I personally like the Taoist methods of seminal retention taught by Mantak Chia and the Healing Tao. But there are many others that teach this. It's a beautiful thing when you can reverse that situation because your vibration gets higher and higher, without much effort.

The Dark Side and the Light Side of Female Sexual Energy

Women do not lose their energy the same way that men do in sex. But there is something that happens with women that causes a blockage as a result of sex that can cause a woman to be in a low-energy, addictive state. And in order to understand that, you have to understand the difference between the way male sexual energy and female sexual energy flows.

If you're just looking at the animal reproductive 'instinctive' state, then male sexual energy naturally flows *out* of the body. Female sexual energy flows *into* the body. For women, the energy naturally flows from the sexual organs up into the body and into the heart. Women lose that energy once a month when they have their period and when they give birth and also when breastfeeding. So that dissipation too can happen in large quantities, all at once, but it's not happening on an ongoing, daily basis as it is for men.

What can happen with women, though, is this:

When a woman is having casual sex with someone they are not connected with, the energy they receive from their partner can sometimes be hostile or aggressive.

And often, when a man ejaculates into a woman and they're feeling anger or aggression, all that anger and aggression goes into the woman. Energetically, without being conscious of it, what a woman will do is block that energy from moving anywhere past their genitals. It won't go into the body because it's negative energy. And her energy system won't allow it to go in. So, the energy is blocked.

So a woman can create a blockage from disconnected sex. And that blockage can also block the flow of her creativity.

Women often talk about creativity, how sometimes they feel their creativity is blocked. Men do too obviously. But since women are the creators of life, then tend to notice more when their creativity is blocked. This block, like all blocks, is happening on an energetic level, often unconsciously.

Women are also capable of having full-body orgasms when energy is flowing freely into their bodies, but once the energy is blocked from moving into the body, it stays only at the genitals level, limiting the experience to a clitoral or 'genital' orgasm.

The genital orgasm is the female version of the addictive orgasm. It's the hormonal response that we become addicted to. We become addicted to the very opiates that we produce during the ejaculation, or the clitoral orgasm. In essence, it's no different than if we were addicted to a morphine or any other type of opiate.

In the limited orgasm state, it's much more likely that we're going to have random, meaningless sex. Maybe with someone we don't even like. That creates even more opportunities for the generation and exchange of negative energy, and all that negative energy creates more blockages.

Clearing Sexual Blocks

As with all other energy blockages, the best way to clear sexual blocks is through visualization and breathing exercises, such as the ones they teach in Tantric schools of thought and also in Taoist sexual practices.

For example, you can breathe into your sexual organs and as that energy starts to build up, bring it into your heart. Feel love and joy in your heart. Bring it into your body. Or circulate it up your spine, down your spine, through all your body, into the ground, up into the sky. In all these different ways you can have your energy channels open and flowing so that you don't have that block anymore.

Simply modify the clearing meditation techniques I've already shown you with the intent of specifically working on sexual blockages.

You might find that when you do clearing exercises that you re-experience trauma or anger or pain. Old, unresolved energies dam up behind blockages. Unblocking will mean that all the trauma that has been stored in your sexual center has to flow through you. There's going to be a period of working through emotional trauma that you may have to experience when you're opening up and clearing that blockage.

But what you'll also find is that once your sexual blockages are cleared, you're going to be much more interested in partners with whom you can have a deeper connection – a deep spirit, mind, heart, full-body, full-soul connection. And when you find a partner like that, for both men and women, it becomes much easier to maintain a clear, high-vibration state of being.

Working Together as Conscious Partners

It's much easier for a man to have an orgasm and pleasure from sex and not ejaculate when he's with a partner that he has a deep connection with. It's much easier for a woman to accept the positive energy of a partner she has a deep connection with. You need a partner that's conscious, you need a partner whose channels are open, and you need a partner that can help you channel that energy when it builds up.

So, if you're working together as partners, here are some things you can do.

The following description assumes a man and a woman working together, but same-sex partners can simply modify the language and the practice to reflect their own experience.

- Either stand or sit facing each other or sit in a way where the woman has her legs folded across the man. Your foreheads are either touching or are very close. And you breathe together. Inhale and exhale at the same time. And visualize what's happening when you inhale and exhale at the same time.
- It doesn't matter too much how you move the energy, what's important is that you're inhaling and exhaling together, and you are visualizing the same movement of energy together.
- An example is that you agree that on the inhale the energy goes from the man's sexual organ up his spine and to his forehead. And then when you exhale, the energy goes from the man's forehead to the woman's forehead down her spine. So you create a circuit of sexual energy that's flowing through both bodies.
- Inhale, up the man's spine, exhale, down the woman's spine. Inhale, up the man's spine. You can do that for a while – five minutes, maybe 10 minutes.

- You can also breathe in and out of different centers. For example, imagine the inhale goes into the man's sexual organs. The exhale goes into the woman's sexual organs – Inhale goes to the man's sexual organs – Exhale goes to the woman's sexual organs. Then work your way up the body. Inhale goes into the man's navel. Exhale goes into the woman's navel. Inhale goes in the man's navel. Exhale goes in the woman's navel. Then work your way up to the heart. Inhale goes to the man's heart. Exhale goes to the woman's heart.
- Then inhale from the throat – inhale into the man's throat, exhale into the woman's throat. And then inhale into the man's eyebrow, third eye, exhale into the woman's third eye.
- It doesn't matter the direction the inhale and the exhale travel. You just have to agree on a joint vision of what's going on.
- You can reverse everything I'm saying. It's just about moving energy to open up the channels. If you look at the gutters on your roof, it doesn't matter which way your hand goes to clear the gutters, you just want to clear the gutters with your hand and get the water flowing in either direction. When energy is flowing, channels are being opened and blocks are being dissolved.
- The key to this is to get a flow going. Flow is the opposite of blocked.
- A variation is that you breathe together and imagine the energy spiraling around both of you and wrapping around you to connect you deeper.

Another Exercise

- Lying down, the man's spooning the woman.
- Inhale – imagining the energy going up the man's spine.

Exhale – imagine it's going down the front of the
woman.

- Inhale – it goes from the woman's sexual organs up the
  man's spine, into the head. Exhale, it goes down the
  woman's front. And you can do this together as you are
  falling asleep. And then turn the other way and have the
  woman spooning the man and do similar visualizations.

By doing these practices, you have the energy channels open and
flowing between the two of you, so that when you do have sex
and one of the partners is about to orgasm, that energy has a
place to go. For men, the energy doesn't have to run out of the
penis – it has another direction that it can flow.

And then when you are making love, breathe together. Try not to
be too mechanical.

Rather than indulging in unconscious, repetitive movements,
look at each other, breathe together, imagine the energy
circulating in and around you both. All the clearing exercises
you practiced when not having sex you can practice during sex
and they will be exponentially more powerful.

And then when things get to the breaking point (for the man)
take a moment and go into a meditative state together. Breathe
together, imagine the energy circulating in and around each
other as best as you can in every direction.

For men, make a conscious effort at this time to bring the energy
up your spine into your head and into your partner, so you can
avoid ejaculating.

What you'll find with practice is you get to a place of relaxation.
And you may feel in your sexual organ the same involuntary
contractions that you feel when you ejaculate, but you don't
actually ejaculate. So what you have is this sort of non-
ejaculatory orgasm. And then when you imagine the energy

going from your forehead into the woman's forehead, and filling her body, she will quite often have a similar orgasmic experience.

And then, after a few minutes of meditating together in this position, you can continue. The beauty of not ejaculating is that you can have sex for as long as you want when you finally master the practice. You can make love for hours at a time or several times a day if you want and the energy never exhausts itself. You never feel tired or dissipated.

Sex practiced this way is a life-changing experience.

But what's also cool is that as incredible as that experience is, you actually don't *need* it. There's no addiction attached to it like there is with unconscious sex. You don't need that addictive hit. You don't need to expel your energy.

Instead, you feel calm and centered, relaxed, energized, powerful, and creative.

These practices are also extremely useful if you're interested in not being sexual at all, for whatever reason.

The virtues of celibacy, chastity and sexual continence have been espoused by religions all over the world since the dawn of time, but unfortunately the applications have been nothing short of horrendous. Widespread abuse and rape of nuns and children by men of the cloth is so commonplace it's often hardly given a second thought. This is true of monks in the West as well as the East. It's tragic and horrific and evil.

I believe the problem is that while monks and priests are *expected* to be celibate, they are not taught *how* to be celibate. Simply put, that sexual energy needs a place to go. The energy channels need to be open and flowing, and the sexual energy needs to be consciously cycled away from the sexual organs, otherwise celibacy simply doesn't work, no matter how well intentioned one may be.

The same principles that apply to conscious sex also apply to celibacy. You can use visualization and breathing exercises to circulate your sexual energy on your own. You don't even have to be in an excited sexual state to do it. You can circulate the energy when it's 'cold'. I've often felt that just a little bit of training for monks and priests is all it would take to end this unfortunate cycle of abuse.

And celibacy, if executed correctly, can be an amazing experience. Because, again, all of the pleasurable feelings of sex already exist inside of us. When we can access them directly, we can be in a perpetual state of bliss. But in order to reap these benefits, it requires deep meditations, visualizations and breathing exercises that will allow us to redirect our sexual energy and access our bliss directly,

Either way, whether you're practicing on your own, with a partner or while being celibate, learning how to circulate your sexual energy is such a powerful way to open your energy channels and raise your vibration.

And that's why bringing consciousness to your sexuality is one of the greatest things you can do to help keep your energy and vibration in the highest state possible.

To learn more about energetic sexual techniques, I recommend The Healing Tao Center and Mantak Chia's teachings. I learned them in 1987 and have been practicing them ever since.

15

OTHER WAYS TO OPEN YOUR CHANNELS

HERE ARE some other things you can do to help open your energy channels...

Fasting/Detoxing: As we've talked about a few times, fasting cleanses your body and your energy channels. I learned this from first-hand experience. It was right after I had been on a 21-day water fast that I had that experience of higher consciousness. Jesus fasted for 40 days and Buddha fasted for six months. Ramakrishna, the Indian spiritual giant of the late 1800s, also fasted for six months while in a superconscious state. While Jesus, Buddha and Ramakrishna are all regarded as divine incarnations by their followers, I believe that it was all the fasting and meditating they did that allowed that divinity to fully express itself in human form. I also believe that 'everyday people' like us have an opportunity to maximize the amount of higher energies we can channel into our bodies by doing the same things they did.

I mentioned earlier that my good friend Robert Peng fasted and meditated in an underground chamber of a Buddhist monastery for 100 days when he was 17 years old. After this experience he acquired the ability to transmit chi energy into his patients to heal their bodies. It's pretty unreal to feel the current of his energy run through your body. It feels like a soothing electric current.

Fasting is not something to be taken lightly. It needs guidance and supervision. If you're interested in learning more about it, I recommend the book *Fasting and Eating for Health* by Dr. Joel Furman.

Other ways to detox include drinking green juice, super greens, spirulina and chlorella, saunas, colonics, detox herbs and exercise.

Exercise: Exercise helps reduce stress, circulate your blood and oxygenate your body. Anything that gets your blood flowing will help get the energy in your life-force channels flowing as well.

Yoga or Stretching: Dawson Church, Ph.D., the energy researcher and author of *The Genie in Your Genes*, says, "The body's connective tissue system is a giant liquid crystal semiconductor". Anything we do that increases the flexibility of our connective tissue will allow for greater energy flow through the body.

Tai chi and Qigong: These systems combine gentle movement, breathing and visualization to open up your energy channels and circulate chi through your system.

Acupuncture: The whole system of acupuncture is based on the belief that all disease is caused by blockages in our energy channels. The needles acupuncturists use help open blockages and get your chi flowing again.

Eating Higher Vibrational Foods: higher vibrational foods are live foods that still have biologically active enzymes and friendly bacteria. They also have captured sunlight in the form of biophotons that interact in positive ways with our DNA. They're also easy to digest and assimilate. These include live (preferably organic) salad greens, sprouts, high water content fruits and cultured foods. Try to add them to your meals as much as possible. The higher your vibration, the higher the vibration of the foods you crave. Ever notice when you're sick you often crave lower vibration foods like sweets, white bread and junk food? It's the exact opposite when you're channeling higher vibrational energies through your body. When you're really feeling alive you crave the live vibrant stuff. This further raises your vibration and creates a positive cycle.

Sunlight: Sunlight is the energetic source of all life on earth. All food comes from plants turning sunlight into macronutrients. The energy we derive from food is actually our way of digesting sunlight. Sunlight also increases vitamin D and reduces inflammation.

You don't want to burn yourself, but there are tremendous benefits to exposing your skin to 10 or 15 minutes of sun every day. Even five minutes is great.

Try standing barefoot on the ground, with the majority of your skin exposed to the sun and imagine breathing the sunlight into your bones and your bones starting to glow with energy. Also imagine this sunlight circulating all through your body and opening up your energy channels. Taoists believe that our bones and the area around our kidneys are places we store energy. So fill up each day if you can with the free and abundant life force of the sun!

Being in Nature and Walking Barefoot in Nature: nature has its own unique chi. Water chi, earth chi, air chi and wood chi all are distinct and nourishing to your energy system. Walking barefoot, also known as 'grounding', has been shown to lower stress and inflammation. It also lets excess energy run through you, which further opens your energy channels. Anytime your energy is moving through your body the channels are being opened.

Clearing Trauma and Emotional Blockages

To the best of my knowledge, no one has ever gotten through life without encountering some form of trauma. A useful definition of trauma is 'anything that compromises your capacity to take effective action'.

While that might seem a little broad, I still think that this is a useful definition.

If you cut your finger, that's trauma. Your finger no longer works as well as it does when it's uninjured, and you need to wait until healing restores your finger to full functionality.

Injury and trauma can happen anywhere in your body. Each time, it compromises the area it affects and reduces your capacity to take effective action.

But there's emotional trauma too, which might or might not affect your body, but which will affect your capacity to act.

If you had, say, a very scary experience with spiders as a child, you might have experienced an emotional trauma that keeps you scared of spiders. This might not cause you too many problems if you live a life where you seldom encounter spiders. But just imagine one day you're driving, and you suddenly notice a spider, in your car, on the windshield.

A person who has no fear of spiders might make a conscious decision, with purposeful intent, simply to brush the spider away, or to live and let live. But if you have a fear of spiders you might panic. Conscious, purposeful intent flies out the window and you lose control of your car and you have an accident. That accident might be so terrible, so traumatic, that you never get into a car again. This example shows us that trauma can have long-lasting effects and can keep us in fearful, low energy, low consciousness and, as a result, we do unconscious, reactive things that get us into more trouble, more trauma and affect our capacity to act.

Emotional trauma causes blockages in our energy channels. You know how when you've experienced trauma or abuse you don't want to think about it or talk about it? You basically don't want to 'go there'. It's almost like there's a block in our conscious mind that prevents us from thinking about or talking about the incident. And when we do talk about it, we often experience all the pain, fear and negative emotions all over again.

When the trauma is so great, we dissociate and sometimes have no conscious recollection of the event at all. *No memory whatsoever*. It's as if the experience has been completely blocked from your consciousness. Well, whenever there is a block in your consciousness, it will manifest as a block in your energy channels, somewhere in your body.

In the 2017 movie *King Arthur: Legend of the Sword*, Arthur is unable to channel the energy of the sword at first. Every time he picks it up he sees a painful memory of the death of his parents. It's so painful that he doesn't want to look at it. It's a trauma that he's dissociated himself from and doesn't even have any memory of. It's been 'blocked' from his consciousness.

Every time he picks up the sword he gets a vision of the memory and he lets go, because he doesn't want to see it. Eventually he's able to see the whole traumatic scene in its entirety and it's only then that he can hold onto the sword and channel its energy.

This is a brilliant metaphor for life because it's only after we've healed all our childhood trauma and our channels are fully open and flowing that we can channel enormous energy and power into our bodies and out into our lives.

Stress and trauma also cause us to have negative emotions and negative emotions also cause blockages in our energy channels.

For this reason, working through past emotional trauma and current stressful situations is essential for keeping your energy channels open and flowing.

We all have trauma. Ramakrishna once said that life is like wearing a white suit in a coal mine. It's impossible not to get dirty, no matter how careful you are. And the same is true for emotional trauma. No matter how careful we are, no matter how loving and supportive our parents, teachers and nurturers have been, and no matter how much we try to avoid being hurt, we all have suffered trauma.

Of course, sometimes our parents, teachers and caregivers are not so careful. Sometimes they are intentionally cruel and abusive. Either way, trauma is part of life and learning how to heal is essential.

Fortunately, because trauma sucks so much, people have been working on various ways of dealing with the effects of trauma and how to heal ourselves.

We need the right tools to work through trauma, tools that work for us as individuals, because trauma can get very specific and personal, and there's no 'one size fits all' answer for a path to healing.

Some of the methods I've used for healing trauma are:

Meridian Tapping
Cellular Release
Regression Therapy
Past life regression
Ancestral healing
EMDR
Soul Retrieval
And Journaling

This is just a small list. Feel free to google each of them and see which ones feel right to you.

I'm kind of a healing junkie and I'm usually willing to try any type of therapy that promises benefit. I treat emotional healing like personal hygiene. It's something that needs to be done every day, or at least several times a week. It's not like getting your car fixed, where a one-off session is all you need. I treat it as a way of life. I currently have an energetic healer that I work with twice a week. She does her sessions remotely and the shifts I experience are pretty amazing.

Eventually, with persistence, we can deal with a lot of our trauma. But life continues to happen to us and, with it, the risk of trauma.

We might still be wearing a white suit, but if we wash it every day we can keep it clean, and keep our energy channels clean too.

Experiencing Higher Vibrational Emotions – In the same way that lower emotions block your energy channels, higher vibrational emotions unblock your energy channels and get your energy flowing. Try this when you're meditating:

Imagine every cell of your body is saying the following words over and over...

I Love You
I Appreciate You
I Forgive You
I Accept You

If you try it now you can see how quickly your emotional and energetic state changes.

Also any acts of charity, kindness or selfless service generate higher emotions.

Doing any kind of art, dancing, or simply doing anything you love, just for fun, is also a great way to generate higher vibrational emotional states.

Breaking Addictions: Addictions lower our energy. Addictions to harmful substances like drugs and alcohol are particularly problematic. When we're under the influence we are less able to protect ourselves energetically. Let me elaborate on this just a little bit.

We have an energetic bubble around us that protects us from lower consciousness, non-physical beings. This bubble is sometimes referred to as our aura. My experience is that we have seven, concentric bubbles around us. It's like a Russian doll, with one bubble smaller than the next.

When our consciousness is compromised while under the influence of drugs, alcohol or even during general anesthesia, our aura is also compromised. Lower energetic beings can attach themselves to our aura and begin feeding off of us. They can even influence our behavior, causing us to crave the harmful substance more, so they can better control us. This creates a vicious cycle that lowers our energy and keeps us trapped in a negative spiral.

It shouldn't be too surprising at this point that we have an aura we can't see or that there are non-physical beings we can't see. We know now that we only see a very small percentage of energies in the universe. About one ten-thousandths of the energy in the universe is visible. And while we can detect lots of other energies with instruments, we can't detect it *all*. So if we can't see it or detect it, it's just not there as far as we're concerned. *But it is there.*

There are many more non-physical beings in this universe than there are physical ones. Some are more evolved than us. Those beings are loving and helpful. Others are less evolved and some of the less evolved ones are parasitic and seek to live off our energies. It's definitely in our best interest to keep our energetic aura as strong as possible. Having your energy channels open and flowing and channeling higher energies is the best way to protect yourself, because those beings can't go anywhere near the higher energies that you can channel. It's like a moth getting too close to a raging fire. It may be attracted to the light, but the light is too bright and too hot for them to tolerate.

One of the reasons why we do drugs in the first place is to escape the pain of past emotional trauma. So one great way to break the vicious cycle of this kind of addiction is to start by doing work to heal past trauma. Also meditation will access the same pleasurable parts of the brain that drugs do. The combination of meditation, prayer, and trauma work is pretty powerful for breaking addictions.

Visualization is also very effective for breaking addictions. What you can do is imagine yourself engaging in the activity and imagine a really negative experience. For example, I was able to break an addiction to smoking as a teenager by imagining I was smoking and the cigarette tasted and smelled like the tar they use to make roads. I imagined touching the cigarette to my mouth and instantly spitting it out because it tasted so bad.

We use this technique all the time at *The Gabriel Method* to break food addictions. You can imagine sugar being ground glass and chocolate being … ah … something really disgusting that looks like chocolate. It's super effective because the body doesn't know the difference between a real and imagined experience. So when you visualize something happening, your body takes it as real. If you'd like to break an addiction, give it a try. Sometimes it only takes one negative visualization to do the job.

Prayer and Asking for Guidance: God, our higher self, our spirit, soul, guides, guardian angels, helpers – however you want to think of it – these benign, benefic influences are always available to us. We just have to ask. Ask God and or your higher self to open up your energy channels and radiate higher energies into your body. I do after every meditation. I say "God and higher self, please open up my energy channels and radiate your love and light into this body and out into the world according to your will and your agenda" and that's how I start every day. I recommend it highly!

16

ONE SIMPLE HABIT!

Let's sum up what we've talked about so far:

- The world probably isn't real. It's most likely some highly advanced computer simulation. That doesn't answer the question of who we really are and why we're playing this simulation, but nonetheless, it's most likely true.
- Even if the world is 'real' it is ABSOLUTELY NOTHING like the way we see it. We're 99.99 percent empty space. Light is not 'light'. Dark is not 'dark'. There's no colors, no sound, no smells, no cold, no heat and nothing is solid. It's all just different waves of energy that our mind and senses turn into the illusion of a real, solid world.
- The waves of energy that make up our bodies and the rest of the world are also moving forward and backwards in time and can be both in this universe and in any number of parallel universes simultaneously.
- Since we are made of these same particles, we can also be 'here' in this world and this universe or in any number of parallel universes simultaneously.

- The idea that parallel universes exist is no longer just a theory. Google and the U.S. Department of Defense now have fully functioning quantum computers that take advantage of parallel universes in their processing. In 2019, Google's computer proved 'quantum supremacy' and solved a problem in three and a half minutes that would otherwise take the fastest computers in the world 10,000 years to solve.
- Our brains and mind are fully equipped to create a COMPLETELY FALSE reality for us and there would be no way for us to know.
- We see ourselves as solid beings in a world with other solid things and beings traveling through time in one direction from past to future.
- While this is completely false based on what we know, our brains are nonetheless creating this illusion for us all the time.
- As part of creating this illusion, our senses, brains and minds filter out the vast majority of real information in the world, such as radio waves, microwaves, ultra violet, x-ray and gamma radiation, dark matter, life force or chi energy – basically 99 percent of the energy in the known universe we cannot see, smell, feel or touch.
- We're also living on a planet that's spinning at a rate of 1,000 miles per hour, traveling around the sun at 67,000 miles per hour and around the galaxy at 450,000 miles per hour and the galaxy is traveling at around 1,600,000 miles per hour and we don't feel any of it.
- One of the MANY things that our senses, brains and minds filter out is the fact that we are continually traveling through different parallel universes all the time.
- If we examine our memories closely, we may find evidence that we are in a slightly different universe

currently to the one we grew up in. Millions of people have collectively found examples of different or false memories (Magic Mirror on the wall). The phenomenon is called the Mandela Effect.

- Based on the evidence we just discussed, and my own experiences and moments of realization, I've come to the conclusion that we are moving through universes all the time, seamlessly, moment by moment, without realizing it.

- That we are living in an infinite ocean of universes one stacked upon the next. Imagine an infinite number of horizontal lines, one stacked on top of the next, going up to the sky. Each horizontal line in the analogy represents a universe – a 'timeline'.

- It's my opinion that this 'ocean of universes' we are living in behaves very similar to an ocean of water. The more hard, cold and dense the universe is, the lower it is in this 'ocean of universes'. The lower the vibration of the universe, the lower it is in the ocean of the universes. The lighter, brighter and more beautiful the universe – the higher the vibration of the universe – the higher it is in the ocean of universes.

- The way to live in the higher, lighter, more vibrant and more beautiful universes is to raise your energy or your vibration, to match those universes. The same way a hot-air balloon will float higher when you raise the vibration of the air inside the balloon. Or the way a scuba diver will float higher in an ocean by inflating his buoyancy compensator (a type of balloon).

- If we can raise our energy and vibration we will effortlessly float up to the higher universes.

- The solution to all of our problems AND the world's problems already exist in higher vibrational universes.

- Therefore, the way to solve all your problems AND the

world's problems is to take steps to raise your energy and vibration and travel to the universes where these problems are already solved.

- The way to raise your energy is to open your energy channels, so that higher energies can be channeled into and through your body.

- There are extremely high vibrational energies in the multiverse that we can't see or detect. These include chi or life-force energy, your soul, spirit, higher self and God consciousness energies. These energies can only come into your body if your energy channels are open and flowing. They simply won't and can't enter your body if your channels are blocked. It would be dangerous and damaging to your body and mind.

- The more open your energy channels are the more of these higher energies you can channel into your body and the higher your vibration will be. It's like the difference between a bowling ball in the ocean and a sponge. A bowling ball is dense and solid and will sink to the very bottom of the ocean. When our energy channels are blocked, we become dense on a vibrational level and we sink to lower, denser universes. A sponge has lots of holes for the water to flow through. Its overall vibration is much higher, so it floats. In the same way, when our energy channels are open and flowing, we can channel more of the invisible energy of the universe and we float higher and higher automatically.

- When we're channeling our higher energies better, we also become more inspired, more enthusiastic, more creative and able to live our life's purpose. We become 'channels' for creativity. The word 'inspired' means 'spirit entering the body'. Enthusiasm means 'letting God in'. The mechanism for having our spirit and higher energies enter our body is through our energy channels.

So when they are open and flowing, our higher energies are able to guide us, inspire us and help us channel creativity into the world. We also have better intuition, we're more able to be guided and to live the exact life we are meant to live.

There are several ways to open your energy channels, including:

- The visualizations in this book
- Other forms of mediation focused on circulating energy.
- Healing emotional trauma
- Fasting
- Reprogramming dysfunctional beliefs
- Redirecting and circulating your sexual energy
- Grounding
- Mind–body work like tai chi, qigong and yoga
- Eating higher vibrational foods
- Being in nature

We want to create habits that will open our energy channels, allow us to radiate higher energies into and through our bodies, raise our vibration and allow our higher vibration to effortlessly take us to higher, more beautiful worlds, where we are living a higher, more beautiful, more successful life. We also want to sever the cords that bind us to a lower energy existence and use our intention to guide us to the optimal universe for us.

So let's start with habit *numero uno*:

The most important thing to do, in order to get started, is to practice the Best Universe Possible meditation in chapter 13 or something similar every day.

To listen to a recording of this visualization visit thegabrielmethod.com/bestworld

I'm a big believer in building habits one at a time. To me a habit is like an asset that pays dividends forever. The hard part is creating the habit, but once it's in place, it can yield positive results that affect every aspect of your life, automatically.

You don't have to think about a habit—the behavior is automatic. Your morning routine is to wake up and brush your teeth, and this habit saves you countless thousands of dollars in dental bills and keeps your breath fresh and clean.

In the same way, if you make practicing this specific meditation/visualization a habit it will pay countless dividends in the form of open and flowing energy channels, increased intuition and guidance, higher vibrational energies flowing through your body, raising your vibration, inspiring you to live the life of your dreams and effortlessly taking you to the best life possible in the best world possible.

Then once this mediation is a habit you can move on to some of the other things we talk about, like eating higher vibrational foods, healing your emotional trauma, changing limiting beliefs and cultivating your sexual energy.

From there you may be inspired to do other mind–body practices that further open up your energy channels, like qigong, tai chi or yoga.

Then you may be guided or inspired to make some illogical changes. Your intuition may guide you to change jobs, fields of study, relocate or travel. You will be a higher vibrational version of yourself, living in a higher vibrational world, so the things you did before, the place you're living and maybe even some of the people you associate with may no longer be compatible with your new vibration. That's OK. Trust your intuition, trust your guidance, trust your vibrations, trust the higher energies that are running through your body, trust your new universe and trust your quantum immortality.

You're on a journey that will give new meaning and purpose to your life that you never imagined possible. TRUST YOUR JOURNEY!

But it all starts with building ONE simple habit and making it a habit for life. Commit to yourself now to meditate every day for the rest of your life, even if it's just for two minutes. Meditate every day, no matter what, come rain or come shine. Pretty soon, two minutes will turn into 10 minutes and 10 minutes will turn into 30 minutes.

In a while you simply won't want to start your day until you've been meditating for at least an hour. You'll be hooked. The bliss, the relaxation, the energy, the guidance and connection with your higher self will all compound to create an experience that's so alluring, you'll be looking forward to it as the most productive and most enjoyable time of your day.

I always make time for my meditations. Not out of some kind of feeling of commitment or obligation, but because there is quite simply nothing on earth I would rather do than meditate. I'm addicted. I'm hooked and nothing feels anywhere near as good.

I remember I was traveling once with my videographer. I was supposed to pick him up at 6:00 am one morning to catch a plane. He was staying at his friend's house and I was late. I couldn't find the house. His friend asked, "Do you think Jon overslept?". And he said, "No man, Jon's been up since 3:00 am meditating." And it was true, I was. I don't *love* getting up at 3:00 am. I'd rather sleep later, but I *really* don't enjoy living a day when I haven't meditated.

Even today I woke up at 1:00 am and meditated from 1:00 to 4:00 am. I did that because I knew that my son was going to wake up at around 6 and I had to finish my meditation beforehand. It was an amazing meditation and I'm so glad I did it! I still got four hours' sleep before I started meditating and another two and a half hours of sleep after, so it all worked out perfectly.

I've learned that if I force myself to start my day before I've completed my meditation and before I know that my energy channels are open and flowing, the day sucks!

It would have been better for me if I had just spent the whole day in bed. Things just mess up somehow.

When my energy channels are not fully open and there's a block somewhere, it manifests as a block in my life. Projects I'm working on stall, people are argumentative, I'm more reactive, I say something I regret to someone, or I make a decision that I regret and the whole day is a bust. I become like that chicken without a head we talked about earlier. The divine guidance is not there, the divine energy is not flowing through my body, I'm coming from a place of ego and it just plain sucks.

What you'll notice over time as you practice this meditation or something similar is that there is a definite cause and effect relationship between how well your life is flowing and how well your energy channels are flowing. When you have a really great meditation, you'll see how things just magically work out and resolve themselves in your life, your relationships, your health, your finances, your career and in the world too. It's almost as if your life situation and the state of the world are an out-picturing of your energy and the way it's flowing. And guess what? It is!

When your channels are flowing it leads you to a version of yourself and a version of the world in which your life is flowing and the world is doing better. It's magical to experience, so I would invite you to take notice of this amazing relationship.

Once you see for yourself, firsthand, how things change in your life and the world, there's no going back. You will be firmly living in a new paradigm and will have boundless energy, inspiration and enthusiasm to double and triple your efforts to open your channels and raise your energy. You will be a conscious universe hopper, riding the waves of quantum immortality... well... forever!

It all starts with making just ONE practice a habit and practicing it every day, for the rest of your life...

17

NOWHERE TO GO BUT UP

I'VE ALWAYS LOVED SCIENCE, especially physics. That being said, even though I do love science, my approach to life is distinctly unscientific. While the scientific model says that nothing is true unless proven true and even then, it can only be considered a theory at best, I take a very different approach.

My approach to life is that *everything is true and possible until proven untrue or impossible,* and even then, you can never *ultimately* prove that something is false or impossible. All you can really say about anything is that it's of no useful value – at least for the time being.

In a sense the standard scientific approach and my approach are two sides of the same coin. But the difference between my approach and a conventional scientific approach is that I have always been open to trying things that may be years away from being accepted as a 'scientifically approved', valid concept.

My idea is that I will try anything if it will *benefit* me or others, as long as there are no negative consequences. I've tried lots of stuff. Lots of things have proven to be useless, at least for me, but at the same time, other things have proven to be invaluable.

And those things that have been proven to be invaluable may be years, if not decades, away from being generally acknowledged as scientifically 'valid'.

The contents of this book contain the most valid ideas and practices that I have discovered in over 30 years of experimenting on myself and life. The concepts are, at times, radically different from the *generally accepted* world view. But at the same time, the information is out there and most of us either don't know about it or don't know what to make of it.

I calculate that I've meditated for over 20,000 hours in my life. That being said, I'm not the most experienced meditator in the world and I'm nowhere near the most knowledgeable student of physics.

What I am, though, is a physics student who has probably done more meditating than most physics students and I'm a meditator who has probably learned more physics than most meditators. It's like a Reese's Peanut Butter Cup thing. Someone put chocolate in my peanut butter and someone put peanut butter in my chocolate, and you know what? They taste really great together.

Metaphysics and quantum physics go hand and hand together. They were made for each other and while they might not know it yet, THEY ARE SAYING THE SAME THING!

'Now' is such a beautiful time in history because science and metaphysics are gradually meshing together as one. Listening to a quantum physicist talk about the universe right now is no different than listening to a meditation master that has spent his life meditating in the Himalayas.

They will both tell you, in their own ways, that the world we know is an illusion. It simply does not exist the way we think it does and our senses are lying to us!

I've been fortunate enough to view 'reality' from many angles now. I've also experienced 'totality', in one sudden, life-changing experience. I've played with it on a daily basis, observing the cause and effect of my actions and, at the same time, I've been able to see how the same conclusions I've made are inevitable to the strictly rational, scientific mind.

In a lot of ways, many physicists don't like being physicists right now. The last thing a physicist wants to say is that there's no physical universe or that we're all just waves of energy! The last thing a physicist wants to say is that there are infinite versions of ourselves, living in infinite (and equally 'true', equally 'fake') universes. No physicist wants to say that there's only one electron or other fundamental particle in the entire universe and it's just going backwards and forwards an infinite number of times.

And yet at the same time, some of these conclusions are inescapable using the very same mathematics that make all the 'quantum miracles' possible.

Physicist Sean Carroll, author of *Something Deeply Hidden*, was being interviewed by Joe Rogan. The book talks about the 'many worlds' theory and explains how there are infinite copies of us in an infinite number of parallel universes, pretty much the stuff we've been talking about in this book, minus the practical applications.

In the interview he was asked (and I'm paraphrasing here), "What, if anything, bothers you most about the many worlds idea?" And he said (paraphrasing again), that he "missed the classical version of the universe". He missed looking at things as if they were 'real'. He missed a table being just a table, time moving in one direction and probably most of all, he missed this being the ONLY universe and 'this' (whatever 'this' means), being the ONLY versions of ourselves.

But this idea of a multiverse of infinite universes is where we're all headed.

Five hundred years ago we all thought the sun, planets and stars revolved around the earth. We believed in the 'geocentric' model of the universe. That is, the earth is the center of the universe. Nicolaus Copernicus was the first to suggest the 'heliocentric' model of the solar system, that the earth and planets revolve around the sun.

Like all great renaissance men, he met with great resistance for his forward thinking and revolutionary paradigm shift. He even delayed publishing his theories till after he was dead, to avoid being excommunicated from the church. Kepler and Galileo continued his work and the Catholic Church declared heliocentrism to be 'formally heretical' and banned all books on the subject. Galileo was sentenced to life in prison and died while under house arrest.

It wasn't until Sir Isaac Newton worked out the math that the heliocentric model was accepted. That was more than 100 years after Copernicus' death.

In the same way we're undergoing another revolutionary paradigm shift as we speak. From a '*uni*-verse centric' model to a '*multi*-verse centric' view of existence. Right now, we think our universe is the only universe in existence. We think that everything revolves around 'our' universe.

In reality, our universe is likely nothing more than a drop in the bucket in an infinity of universes we call the 'multiverse'. We're like a drop of water in an ocean of universes.

As I mentioned before, Hugh Everett was the first to propose the idea of 'many worlds' or the multiverse and he was laughed out of the business. Literally, he dropped out of school and never became a physicist because of all the flak he took.

He met with the same predictable resistance as Copernicus and for the exact same reasons. Copernicus suggested that we weren't the center of the universe. And Everett is suggesting that our universe isn't the center of the 'universes' either. Anytime anyone makes an assertion that we're just not that big of deal in the grand scheme of things, it meets with resistance from governments and the scientific and religious communities.

It's the same with ETs. The idea that there are other intelligent beings in the universe threatens our place in the stars. It dilutes our importance and power, so we resist it. It doesn't matter that the Mutual UFO Network (MUFON) has registered over 100,000 UFO sightings and that the U.S. Department of Defense has made public a video of a UFO they admit was not constructed on earth, we still cling to this childish notion that we're the only 'intelligent' life in the universe.

Everett fought the same fight as Copernicus. But just like Copernicus and his heliocentric model, the math of the 'many worlds' model works and is undeniable. It will probably take at least 100 years after Everett's death for the 'many worlds' view to be the generally accepted view of existence, but I say why wait?

Why wait for everyone to put two and two together and figure out that not only are we living in a multiverse with infinite versions of ourselves, but that WE CAN ACTUALLY USE THIS TO OUR ADVANTAGE!

Because I can tell you, *with 100 percent certainty*, that if the ideas in this book are real and valid and useful to you as a person, as a soul, as a traveler, journeying through space time and infinity, then these ideas are YEARS away from being accepted into the mainstream world view.

So, I say why wait? The things I'm suggesting that you do, such as meditate, visualize, heal emotional trauma, cleanse, eat more high vibrational foods, do mind–body practices – these things have no downside.

YOU HAVE NOTHING TO LOSE.

Harvard medicine has said that meditation is possibly the single greatest thing you can do for your health. It reduces stress hormones, increases healing and rejuvenating hormones, reduces inflammation, it lengthens telomerase, it improves concentration, focus, learning, cognitive abilities, neuroplasticity. It reduces depression, addictions... The list goes on and on.

And even if you don't believe that raising our vibration through meditation practices will cause us to transition to higher vibrational universes – even if you believe that there's ONLY one universe that we are living in – meditation can still help improve the one world we are living in.

There have been several studies that show that people meditating in groups can reduce crime, suicide and death in the surrounding areas. One study showed that 4,000 meditators over six weeks reduced the crime rate of Washington D.C. by 23 percent.[1] So even if you're not moving to a more peaceful universe, by practicing the techniques in this book, you are still making yourself better and the world better a better place.

There is no downside!

The only spin I'm putting on it is to add a few steps to the meditation that I believe will help you consciously travel to higher universes. But you know what? If I'm wrong, so what? By trying anyway you've still gained a wealth of mental, emotional, physical and possibly even spiritual benefits. *You have lost nothing.*

It's all gain and no loss.

And if I'm right!

Well, then you get to take advantage of a practice that can help you experience success, prosperity, and abundance IN EVERY ASPECT OF LIFE. A way of being in the world that can help you feel more spiritually connected, have better relationships, be more creative and intuitive, be healthier, more vibrant, more energetic, live your life's purpose more fully, have more financial freedom and possibly even solve many of the world's problems too!

Because let's face it, if I'm right, there's a version of the world where things are better 'out there'. A higher vibrational world where people share more, care more, help more. A place where technologies exist that can remove pollution, generate free energy, solve world hunger and poverty. A place where there are no wars.

The upsides if I'm wrong are great, but the upsides if I'm right are through the roof. The benefits are out of this world! Or, out of this universe to be more precise ;).

With that risk/reward scenario, with that cost/benefit analysis, I can only encourage you with all my heart and soul to give it a try. Practice the simple meditation techniques in this book and the simple concepts. Be patient, be open and rather than focus on the result, simply stay focused on the day-to-day, in-the-moment benefits of practicing these techniques.

Forget about the *end game* and just take it day to day and allow your energy channels to open and your vibration to increase at its own rate.

Don't try to push.

Don't get frustrated when the 'gratification' for a 'future that has not yet happened' isn't 'instant'. Wherever you are at the moment is where you are and just look to make simple, daily improvements to your energy and the quality of your vibration and let the rest take care of itself.

As I've said, the benefits grow exponentially. The amount of improvement you can make in a day, once you're a few years down the road, will be 10 times what you can achieve in a day now. They might even be 100 times greater for you. I don't know.

Take it slow and easy and enjoy your journey to health, happiness, success, prosperity and a deeper connection with the real, infinite all-knowing, all-loving you.

The universes are waiting for you!

ABOUT THE AUTHOR

Jon Gabriel is an international bestselling author and creator of *The Gabriel Method*. His books have been translated into 16 languages and are available in 60 countries around the world.

For a free powerful visualization, visit
thegabrielmethod.com/bestworld

ACKNOWLEDGMENTS

I am grateful for the help, love and support of Xavier Waterkeyn, Inge Tatiana, Rafael Nasser, Grant, Beth and Kaileen Sherk, Leonard, Ethel, Joey, Michelle, Jennifer, Inge and Leo Abrams, Hilary Gans, Lila Thanos, Hariharananda, Prajanananda, Ananda Moi Ma, Ramakrishna, Vivekananada, Sarada Devi, Mahendranath Gupta (M), Guru Mai, Shri Chinmoy, Yogananada, Shri Yukteshwar, Lahiri Mahasaya, Babji, Ramana Maharshi, Michael Gabriel, Emma Mary, Don Abrams, Mantak Chia, Michael Winn, Phoc Phan, Robert and Dongmei Peng, James Colquhoun, Laurentine Colquhoun Ten Bosch, Prince Hugo Maris Gabriel Colquhoun, Rangi Colquhoun, Daphne Motzkin and Khaliah Ali. Without you, this book would be in another universe somewhere waiting to be created.

I would also like to thank Martin Taylor and his team at Digital Strategies for their technical support.

ADDENDUM

You Will Live Forever...

A short story by Inge Tatiana age 17

My hand traced the surface of the river causing ripples that morphed my reflection. I pulled my hand out and let the little ripples fade away back into the clear, still water.

I saw my face, my pale skin, my long, dark-brown hair.

My gaze went back to my full lips and then to the full reflection of me. In my reflection the sun rays penetrated the tops of the canopy of trees I sat under and shone over me as if they made a halo. I heard a voice coming from the other side of the water, an old woman's voice.

"My child, you will live forever. I promise."

I was still staring at my face as a tear fell from my eye.

I did not want to live forever. Not in this life anyway.

I looked up at the old woman. She looked like my mother.

No.

She looked like me ... she is me ...

"A version of you exists in all consciousness and all realities. I am here with you. Do not seek what you choose to live. Choose to live what you seek. That is the law. Everything you wish for is already yours."

I looked down to see my tear in the water, sinking, falling, falling.

I fell on the ground with a loud thump as my eyes opened quickly, startled.

I scrambled onto my hands and knees to look around, half-stunned, and to the people's faces looking at me in shock and horror. I looked down and saw I was unharmed by a sword that had just stabbed me, a sword that should have cut through my flesh. Instead I saw the wound that should have been mine on a tree, which was some fair distance from me.

As if the dream in which I found myself wasn't already a lot to take in, I couldn't help but wonder why I had been left unharmed by the stab wound.

I watched as the king's knight took off his helmet, his eyes wide open.

"She is a witch!" shouted the king.

I was still confused how or why this happened but if I didn't move now, I knew that I wouldn't be alive for very much longer.

I ran towards the tree that had the cut marks that should have been on my body. It was clear that they should have been on me – the cuts matched perfectly. As I ran past it, I tried to ignore them before it made me feel too dizzy or overwhelmed.

Dead leaves cracked beneath my bare feet as I ran. I was losing my breath as I stumbled along the clutter of the many plants and fallen branches that covered the floor of the forest, but the sound of the villagers pursuing me kept me going.

I came to a tall cliff that towered over running water that violently crashed against sharp rocks, randomly placed around the water. The muffled voices of the people in my village became louder and more distinct.

I knew what I had to do.

My feet left the edge of the cliff. I fell through the air in a matter of seconds which felt like hours. Then my feet touched the running water, instantly pulling me in, pulling me under its direction.

I struggled to look up as the force of the water did what it wanted with me. But I saw faces staring down at me as the rip pulled me below the surface. I was pushed up again as if I had been given another chance to gasp for air. My heart sank with both fear and relief as I noticed the villagers walking away, confident in their unspoken assumption that I was soon to be dead.

The water was too strong for me to swim. It felt as though it couldn't decide between sucking me down or pushing me up, but I took advantage of every chance I had to breathe.

My head felt light as the water kept pushing me down further and deeper. This time it wasn't pushing me up enough for me to reach the air at the surface. I was too tired to try to stay afloat.

I gave in to the current and let my body sink. As my eyes closed, I began to remember a vision. I was the teardrop sinking into the water deeper.

The shock of a firm hand grabbing my wrist made my eyes jolt open, but I was too tired to stay conscious. My eyes slowly closed as I was being dragged up and through the strong current of the water.

The old woman's voice from my vision echoed in the darkness of my mind.

"My child, you will live forever," was all I heard until darkness overcame me.

My eyes adjusted to the sight of a calm blue sky above me, covered in soft clouds that moved gently with a quiet and gentle breeze that made the tall, light-green grass tickle my face.

Deep-brown, gentle eyes turned to stare at me as I became more aware of my surroundings. His scruffy shoulder-length brown hair blew wild and free in the breeze as I stared back at his face. It was rough, sharp face but also gentle and feminine. His eyes carried a wide, deep and gentle soul. His skin was tan ... sun kissed.

"I saw what you did," he said firmly, but calmly. "You have mastered the technique, but you still haven't fully learned. You must be careful."

Still confused, I asked, "What do you mean?"

"Come with me" he said and took my hand. He led me to stand up beside with him, allowing me to notice the beautiful meadow I was in. I watched him hold his hand out in front of himself as a huge flash of white light flashed in a blink of an eye. Suddenly we were in front of a small village nestled among towering hills and cliffs that stood high over a clear, blue ocean.

I gasped in awe at the beautiful scene. The sun made the whole town glow and the calm ripples in the ocean sparkle.

"How did we...?" I began to ask, but he cut me off by walking fast into the village.

We walked along a brown-brick-paved path, lightly strewn with small stones that sparkled in the sun. I looked up to see people going about their daily lives, in and out of little brown wood and brick huts, walking around small stalls on carts holding fruits, vegetables and bread. Another of the carts held unique glass bottles holding what appeared to be stones. Some bottles even seemed to hold smoke.

As we walked down the village more people stared at me. They weren't surprised to see me so much as they looked as if they had never seen anyone like me before. As I stared at the faces of the villagers I jumped in surprise as I noticed they were in fact not people but beings that looked like people. They had pointed ears, pointed noses and eyes with sharp, pointed tear ducts. No one's hair was above shoulder length.

Their faces were painted with various dots and lines over and or under their eyes. Most of them had tanned skin and white freckles – a trait I had never seen before.

A little girl stood in front of me. She held a small red crystal in her hand as if she wanted to give it to me. I knelt to pick it up, but then everyone gasped. Instantly, the boy who was guiding me turned around. His eyes widened as a shocked expression took over his face.

"You can see them?!" he asked. But even as he spoke my hand had reached out to pick up the crystal. Instead, my fingers went right through the crystal and I fell backwards in both shock and terror as I tried to scramble away in panic.

The boy had come from behind me and picked me up from under my arms and helped me back onto my feet. So many thoughts flooded my mind but all that I managed to say was, "Wait! What?!"

The boy looked down, "She's more powerful than I thought," he muttered to himself.

This was all too overwhelming. One minute I'm just an orphan in a village no one cares about. The next I'm a witch? I'm having visions? No ... I'm delusional!

There's a reason the other kids never liked me or thought I was weird when I was little. Everyone was scared because I was somehow always able to just "have" whatever I needed when I needed it. Then one day the king accused me of stealing and sentenced me to death.

"Look, I ...", I began, but the boy cut me off.

He looked at me. "You're not seeing the reality of my village, are you?"

"What?" I asked in confusion.

"Hold on," he said.

He put his index and middle finger on my forehead. I felt a strong force that felt like a magnet pulling just my forehead forward. It was so strong I couldn't keep my eyes open. I closed my eyes until the force stopped and then I opened them. I saw the exact same scenery but with minor differences. The homes seemed fuller, cluttered with things like wind chimes and handmade decorations woven from sticks and rocks and shells.

More houses contained stained-glass windows here. It looked greener. And when I looked around, I noticed the people appeared more like the boy, tanned skin, long scruffy brown hair.

"Come on! I need to take you to the temple. My master can explain everything."

Once we arrived at what seemed to be the biggest oak tree I had ever seen, I noticed there was a door in front of it. I was in awe when it opened, and I saw a whole little home inside of it with strings of shells hanging from a window and jars that held moss and mushrooms on the window sill.

The boy knelt and spoke into the room. "Master, this girl has mastered The Technique we have practiced for centuries, but she doesn't know how to control it. We must educate her."

He was cut off by a kind and soothing voice...

"Hello!"

As I stared at the detailed ink painting on the walls, I noticed a short old woman with long grey hair walk in from the other side of the room. Her hair was black at the ends.

I looked over to see her face more clearly as she walked out of the light from the sun.

She smiled at me softly. As I was about to introduce myself...

"No need," she said. "Trust me. I've already heard it thousands of times before. In fact, I'm still hearing it! 'Hi! My name's Lilly Belle. My name's Lilly Belle! Nice to meet you! My name's Lilly Belle, but people call me "Belle."' Honestly! It gets a little old, don't you think?" She said this with a laugh, but I was confused. Was this some sort of joke? I didn't get it.

When she looked at me, it was as though she could read my thoughts. She rolled her eyes, "All right. I'll tell you one more time! But this is the last time, understood?" and she proceeded to laugh again. I still didn't get it. Once she settled down, she continued.

She looked deep into my eyes. "Everything you see, touch and feel in this universe isn't real," she said. "It's all just a creation of our own realities. Nothing is truly 'physical', therefore there are infinite realities and possibilities of who you can be and what you want to experience. Knowing this, my people have tried for centuries to master The Technique of travelling through timelines and realities. You ... are so ... uneducated in The Technique and yet you have mastered it so well without even trying, I do wonder what you truly are."

I sat down. "So, you're saying nothing is real?" I asked in disbelief.

"Yes, but everything is real too."

I continued to stare at her "I'll give you an example." She continued. "Remember when, in your hometown the king was going to sentence you to death for just always having food when you needed it, even though your town was in great poverty…"

"Yes," I said. "Wait! How do you…?"

"Well, look at it this way," she continued. "Your energy was so high because your true nature is so loving and kind. You attracted good things into your conscious reality."

I stared at her even more.

She continued. "And because there are multiple timelines, when the king sentenced you to death for stealing, you switched to one where he was standing in front of a tree instead of standing in front of you … and then you switched back."

I then began to believe her. "If that's true, how did I do that?"

"You're a very special girl," she said. "I'll show you both more tomorrow." The sun is setting. "For now, we must rest."

The boy and I walked out of the door. I felt so excited, so *fascinated* I just wanted to know more. I was jumping and spinning around in the grass feeling as if this moment was infinite.

"You seem really happy," the boy said with a smile.

"I just can't believe this is real!" I replied. "What's your name?!" I asked. Before he could say anything else, he stared at me for a second and then burst out laughing, "Ahahaha! This is so overdue! I can't believe I didn't tell you my name!" He said with a big smile.

"Well, better late than never. Am I right?" I responded nervously.

He giggled. "My name is Sol," he said.

Sol? I thought as I stared into his eyes.

He grabbed my arm, interrupting my train of thought, and we ran through the fields towards the forest. Despite everything that happened I felt more alive than I had ever felt before. As we ran, I felt as though we could have been flying. But I began to tire. I pulled him down as we were running. "I'm out of breath," I said as I sat down. He sat down next to me. We were by a pond between the trees as the sun was setting in the distance.

I watched the wind blow the tops of the trees until I turned to see he was watching me... watching the trees. I stared back at him. The sun behind his hair made the loose strands shine gold.

I noticed a small speck of yellow in the corner of my eye. I turned to look at it and gasped. "Oh! A firefly!"

"You've never seen a firefly?" He asked in a jokingly shocked voice.

"No, I haven't!" I said as I stood up as hundreds of fireflies revealed themselves. As the sun left the sky, I was amazed by how many there were and how beautiful they were.

"I will never understand you!" Sol said with a smile.

"What?" I asked.

"After everything you've been through, *this* is what you're most amazed about!?"

I just stared at him. "But look how cute he is!" I said pointing to the firefly.

Sol just laughed.

"You know what I want to do?" I said.

"What?"

"Dance!" I responded and grabbed him.

I was in his arms and we moved like we were dancing at an aristocrat's party in a ballroom, but the field we were in was better. Much better.

I decided I wanted to lie down again. He followed me.

"Gosh, can you make up your mind?" he asked.

"I'm tired," I said with a laugh.

He jokingly rolled his eyes and then looked sad. I immediately knew something was up.

"What's wrong?" I asked

"There's something I need to show you," he said, sounding upset. I began to feel concerned.

"Travelling through timelines isn't always the best thing. And it's definitely not a skill you'd want to exploit too often." He sighed. "Let me show you."

He took my hand then held his hand out too. With the same bright flash of light, we switched timelines and locations. We were somewhere different, but not stunning or beautiful like before.

We were among huge, tall rectangular structures with big reflective windows. I stared at them in curiosity.

"They're called skyscrapers," he said.

We walked along a straight path, but it wasn't vibrant. It was dull and grey, and people dressed in grey with grey faces walked shoulder to shoulder past each other as if anyone besides themselves was irrelevant. Everyone seemed to be in a hurry.

A man accidentally walked into someone and knocked him over. Instead of asking if he was all right, the first man just said, "Hey! Watch where you're going!"

I went up to the fallen man. "Are you OK?" I asked.

"Ugh! Scumbag!" the man mumbled to himself as he picked himself up and walked off.

"He can't see us," Sol said.

"Here," he said as he grabbed my hand and jumped up. We smoothly glided high into the air. We landed on the railing of one of the balconies of a skyscraper and looked through a window. I was looking at a middle-aged woman with tan skin and similar hair to Sol's but tied back. Her hair looked messy. She was wearing a cardigan and sweatpants. She looked tired. She had bags under her eyes. She opened an orange bottle with a white cap and swallowed two pills.

"That's my mother," Sol said. "Although she doesn't know it."

"What?"

"It's complicated," he said.

I wondered why she looked so unhappy. I couldn't think of any other reason other than this feeling that it was because this particular world seemed to simply not care for the people who lived in it.

Sol continued. "She's trapped in this timeline. She can't break free because she is unhappy. I watch her every now and then. She's trapped here. All these people are.

That man you saw fall over earlier? Every single time he falls over the exact same way. They are living the exact same day and they don't even know it. Look, my mother will get a bowl of cereal then she will walk to work. Her boss will yell at her for being late and she will have a panic attack in a room all by herself with no one to help her. She will then calm herself down like nothing happened and go back to her job where she gets yelled at all day. It's just too much with all the commitments she makes and all the bills she has to pay and she's so worried about the debt she's in. It kills me to see her this way, especially when I know the way out for her is so simple."

We flew through the windows and walls and watched as his mother walked down the stairs of her dark, shady room and down the street. We watched her cross the road when I noticed a little rat scurry around me instead of through me.

That's strange, I thought no one in this world could see me.

Just as I was about to continue walking, I tripped over a crack in a grey stone path and fell over. Everyone instantly stopped and stared at me.

Oh no!

I sensed that my presence was an intrusion, that I was interrupting their timeline.

I looked over at Sol's mother. She had stopped in the middle of the road to look at me. A red metal box on wheels was coming towards her. It was all too fast, but it was my fault. I had interrupted her timeline. I had to stop it. Out of instinct I jumped and watched as the front of the red box came towards me. It seemed like it took hours to hit me, but I was powerless to stop it.

Instantly everything went blank.

There were visions and whispers in my head again.

The woman's voice, "My child, you will live forever."

The teardrop.

I woke up, confused.

I looked over and saw that I was on the side of the road.

I saw Sol lying on the road.

I knew he was dead.

Lying there in front of the car that was meant to hit me, panic struck me as I ran over as quickly as I could.

Tears flooded my eyes.

No ... no ... no ...

He had switched realities to one where he was the one that ran in front of the car and I was the one that stayed safe on the pavement. I watched in pain as the woman turned Sol over and cried. She might have been crying because she had almost died. She might have been crying because she was overwhelmed and seen someone die in front of her. But I knew deep down she was crying because on some level she knew who he really was ... her son.

Sol was dead. There was nothing I could do. I just kept running in the city until I was far enough away from where the accident had happened. I found myself on a small patch of grass in a field that was nowhere near as big or majestic as any of the other worlds I had experienced.

And as I lay on the grass under the infinite sky that once felt like it was made just for the two of us to look at, I felt Sol's presence so strongly.

And I *knew* the bigger picture.

We are not male or female.

We are not young or old.

We're not even alive ... or dead.

We are neither anything nor nothing.

We are both simply the same vibration, the same energy, the same consciousness.

We exist in the universe as one and I will never exist without him and I closed my eyes to breathe that feeling in.

I opened my eyes and with a shock I was standing in front of the old woman again and my heart felt content but overwhelmed with happiness as I saw Sol standing next to me. I was dumbfounded.

Had that been a dream too?

The old woman smiled at me.

"That is life," she said. It's all just another dream. Another world. Another reality."

I wondered if Sol experienced what I experienced too.

As I looked over at him, I saw a woman walk in. She stood tall, like a warrior or a goddess. I was so struck by her immense beauty that I didn't immediately recognize her.

"My son, you have found a beautiful woman," she said.

I gasped... it's Sol's mother! And I looked over to see the old woman smiling at me.

As our eyes locked, I felt a tremendous current of peace, joy and bliss pass through my body.

And I could hear that familiar voice in the distance saying, "My child you will live forever."

NOTES

3. YOU'RE VIRTUALLY THERE!

1. 2016 Isaac Asimov Memorial Debate: 'Is the Universe a Simulation?': https://www.amnh.org/explore/news-blogs/podcasts/2016-isaac-asimov-memorial-debate-is-the-universe-a-simulation

4. ROCK SOLID EVIDENCE

1. Everything is mostly empty space: https://www.sciencealert.com/99-9999999-of-your-body-is-empty-space
2. The average atom: https://www.factmonster.com/dk/encyclopedia/science/atoms
3. Fitting everyone into a sugar cube: https://www.scienceabc.com/pure-sciences/can-the-entire-human-race-fit-inside-a-sugar-cube.html
4. A collection of empty spaces: https://www.sciencealert.com/99-9999999-of-your-body-is-empty-space
5. Quantum tunnelling: https://en.wikipedia.org/wiki/Quantum_tunnelling
6. Wave particle duality: https://en.wikipedia.org/wiki/Wave%E2%80%93particle_duality
7. Quantum entanglement: https://en.wikipedia.org/wiki/Quantum_entanglement
8. Quantum superposition: https://www.space.com/2000-atoms-in-two-places-at-once.html
9. Wave probability functions: https://en.wikipedia.org/wiki/Wave_function
10. Virtual particles: https://en.wikipedia.org/wiki/Virtual_particle
11. Multiverse: https://en.wikipedia.org/wiki/Multiverse
12. Einstein and quantum physics: https://www.bbvaopenmind.com/en/temas/einsteins-love-hate-relationship-with-quantum-physics/
13. Time dilation: https://en.wikipedia.org/wiki/Time_dilation
14. Just one electron in the universe: https://en.wikipedia.org/wiki/One-electron_universe
15. Our universe as a hologram: https://futurism.com/what-if-our-universe-hologram
16. The universe as a giant neural network: https://www.dailymail.co.uk/sciencetech/article-8723239/Physics-controversial-theory-argues-entire-universe-neural-network.html

5. FRANCIS JOSEPH COPENHAGEN AND THE DOUBLE-SLIT EXPERIMENT

1. The double-slit experiment: https://en.wikipedia.org/wiki/Double-slit_experiment
2. https://en.wikipedia.org/wiki/Wheeler%27s_delayed-choice_experiment
3. Many-worlds interpretation: https://futurism.com/the-many-world-interpretation-or-the-copenhagen-interpretation
4. Chinese quantum computer: https://www.sciencealert.com/china-has-developed-the-fastest-and-most-powerful-quantum-computer-yet
5. Max Tegmark on quantum computing: https://www.youtube.com/watch?v=bJpIclDmi2M
6. David Deutsch, *The Fabric of Reality*: https://www.goodreads.com/book/show/177068.The_Fabric_of_Reality
7. David Deutsch lectures on quantum computation: https://www.youtube.com/watch?v=24YxS9lo9so
8. 'Gravity's mystery may prove our multiverse exists': https://www.engadget.com/2019/07/13/hitting-the-books-the-trouble-with-gravity/
9. Number of atoms in the universe: https://www.universetoday.com/36302/atoms-in-the-universe/
10. Quantum immortality: https://simple.wikipedia.org/wiki/Quantum_immortality

6. MR. MANDELA AND THE MAGIC MIRROR

1. Rabbi discussing Isaiah 11:6: https://www.youtube.com/watch?v=go6mzqhkLtU
2. Discussion with biblical scholar about Isaiah 11:6: https://www.youtube.com/watch?v=lINs6wNNbZ0
3. Quiz regarding Isaiah 11:6: https://www.youtube.com/watch?v=lINs6wNNbZ0
4. Snow White Magic Mirror scene: https://www.youtube.com/watch?v=Br0DCEEBplY
5. Carpool karaoke, 'We are the Champions': https://www.youtube.com/watch?v=a5MclE7A9EE
6. 'We are the Champions', waiting for the final phrase: https://www.youtube.com/watch?v=a5MclE7A9EE
7. *The Wizard of Oz*, scarecrow's gun: https://www.youtube.com/watch?v=3X8yS2DYVPY
8. Ed McMahon and Publishers Clearing House: https://www.forbes.com/sites/larissafaw/2012/11/21/the-curious-case-of-ed-mcmahon-and-the-publishers-clearing-house/#3172ad8f1b70
9. Ed McMahon and delivering checks: https://www.youtube.com/watch?v=eD8EvB1L84M
10. Ed McMahon and excited woman: https://www.youtube.com/watch?v=D96-Fpg37b4

11. Ed McMahon on the *Roseanne* show: https://www.youtube.com/watch?v=dUqMJG-RfT8
12. Johnny Carson and Ed McMahon: https://www.youtube.com/watch?v=BOYJmN7teww
13. Johnny Carson delivering check to David Letterman: https://www.youtube.com/watch?v=aYrjrlMh_Rg
14. *Portrait of Dorian Gray* from an online bookstore listing.
15. *The Portrait of Dorian Gray* in *The Seven Year Itch*: https://www.youtube.com/watch?v=WZXBP6g9Ovs
16. Woman describing *The Portrait of Dorian Gray* as her favorite book: https://www.youtube.com/watch?v=KNzdj5tS4kg
17. James Earl Jones: https://www.youtube.com/watch?v=GQ1mmkKb_BQ
18. Mark Hamill: https://www.youtube.com/watch?v=dz2UnciOIfI
19. Darth Vader and Luke: https://www.youtube.com/watch?v=bv20ZoBcdO8
20. Mona Lisa's smile: https://mandelaeffect.net/did-mona-lisa-smile/
21. Art student and Mona Lisa's smile: https://www.reddit.com/r/MandelaEffect/comments/96i3ej/how_i_remembered_the_mona_lisa/?utm_source=amp&utm_medium=&utm_content=post_body
22. PhotoShopped *Mona Lisa*: https://i.imgur.com/b12AoAB.jpg
23. Japanese bombing U.S. mainland: https://www.entitymag.com/mandela-effect-examples/
24. https://duckduckgo.com/?q=fruit+of+the+loom+cornucopia+proof&atb=v183-1&iax=images&ia=images&iai=https%3A%2F%2Fi.imgur.com%2FnGVVA43.jpg
25. https://i5.walmartimages.com/asr/35b2f747-2b3b-48a8-977c-ccae7cb16c32_1.29fb32a4075d3a78d3e928d56c02a39e.jpeg
26. Article on Fruit of the Loom: https://imgur.com/a/Au42qr8
27. Nick Hinton and Fruit of the Loom: https://ruinmyweek.com/weird/mandela-effect-fruit-of-the-loom-logo-cornucopia/
28. Woman's bible with 'wineskins': https://www.youtube.com/watch?v=ZrwP8f6onzM
29. Mandela Effect list: https://www.alternatememories.com/mandela-effect-list

10. GETTING THE GUIDANCE YOU NEED

1. Office of Naval Research Basic Research Challenge – Enhancing Intuitive Decision Making Through Implicit Learning; Solicitation No. 12-SN-0007 (July 31, 2012): www.fbo.gov/index?s=opportunity&mode=form&tab=core&id=723de7fc46213a209552d9131dcf2132&_cview=
2. PRWeek: CEO Survey 2006, Burson-Marsteller: media.haymarketmedia.com/archives/1/2006ceosurvey_305.pdf.
3. McCraty, R., et. al., "Electrophysiological Evidence of Intuition: Part 1. The Surprising Role of the Heart," *Journal of Alternative and Complementary Medicine* 10, no. 1 (February 2004): 133–143.

11. A SIMPLE VISUALIZATION TO RAISE YOUR VIBRATION

1. Multiple discovery: https://en.wikipedia.org/wiki/Multiple_discovery

13. SEVERING THE CORDS THAT HOLD US DOWN

1. Milton, G.W., "Self-Willed Death or the Bone-Pointing Syndrome," *Lancet 1*, no. 7817 (June 23, 1973): 1435–1436.
2. Story related by Wayne Dyer in Hay House Radio interview.

17. NOWHERE TO GO BUT UP

1. https://www.worldpeacegroup.org/washington_crime_study.html
    https://guardianlv.com/2014/04/research-shows-group-meditation-can-reduce-crime-rates/
    http://thespiritscience.net/2015/06/18/studies-show-group-meditation-lowers-crime-suicide-deaths-in-surrounding-areas/